The Truth about Special Education

A Guide for Parents and Teachers

Robert Evert Cimera

A SCARECROWEDUCATION BOOK

The Scarecrow Press, Inc.
Lanham, Maryland, and Oxford
2003

A SCARECROWEDUCATION BOOK

Published in the United States of America
by Scarecrow Press, Inc.
A Member of the Rowman & Littlefield Publishing Group
4720 Boston Way, Lanham, Maryland 20706
www.scarecroweducation.com

PO Box 317
Oxford
OX2 9RU, UK

British Library Cataloguing in Publication Information Available

Library of Congress Cataloging-in-Publication Data

Cimera, Robert E.
  The truth about special education : a guide for parents and teachers / Robert
Evert Cimera.
     p. cm.
"A ScarecrowEducation book."
Includes bibliographical references (p.   ) and index.
  ISBN 0-8108-4484-2 (alk. paper) — ISBN 0-8108-4485-0 (pbk. : alk. paper)
  1. Special education—United States—Handbooks, manuals, etc. 2. Children
with disabilities—Education—United States—Handbooks, manuals, etc. I.
Title.
  LC3981 .C56 2003
  371.9'0973—dc21
                                                                2002008134

♾™ The paper used in this publication meets the minimum requirements of
American National Standard for Information Sciences—Permanence of
Paper for Printed Library Materials, ANSI/NISO Z39.48-1992.
Manufactured in the United States of America.

I would like to dedicate this book to Nixon, Dante, Truman, Becky, and especially Agnew.

Contents

Preface

Enrolling a child in special education can be a very scary process, for both the student and the rest of the family as a whole. To help you and your child minimize the inevitable anxiety and to help your child benefit the most they can from special education, this book will help you understand:

- What special education is
- How it differs from regular education
- The legal rights and responsibilities associated with have a child in special education
- How to develop effective educational plans
- Strategies for building effective educational teams
- Basic information regarding common disabilities, and
- Where to find additional information and resources.

I hope that this book helps you and your children. Please remember that special education does not mean "stupid"!

Acknowledgments

I would also like to thank the wonderful people at the University of Illinois, CHADD, CEC, TASH, and Scarecrow Education for their support and assistance.

Special thanks to Frank Rusch, Janis Chadsey, Daizey, and my incredible students.

Please support your local humane societies and have your pets spade or neutered.

CHAPTER 1

An Introduction to Special Education

CHAPTER OBJECTIVES

Upon completing this chapter, you should be able to:

1. Define special education.
2. Contrast special and regular education.
3. Discuss the history of special education.
4. Indicate who is served via special education.
5. Describe the potential effects of special education on family members of students.
6. Name a famous person with a disability.

CASE STUDY: MICHAEL EVERTT AND SPECIAL EDUCATION

"I am glad that you were able to make it," Ms. Roush said as she drew up two chairs for Mr. and Mrs. Evertt in her now empty classroom. The students had gone home a couple hours ago, but she stayed behind to meet with Michael Evertt's parents.

"Is there anything wrong?" Mrs. Evertt asked, the concern showing in her face and voice.

"Well, no." Mrs. Roush hesitated for a moment. "Not really wrong. But I do have concerns about Michael. You see," Mrs. Roush put some of Michael's writing assessments on the table in front of them, "he is still reversing many of his letters and he is having difficulty learning how to read."

Mrs. Evertt looked a bit perplexed. "But last time we met, you said that he was just a little bit behind and that there was nothing to worry about," she said.

"Yes, that was true. I had a couple of other teachers observe my class and suggest ways that I could teach him better, but nothing seems to be working. We are concerned that Michael might have a learning disability."

"A disability!" Mrs. Evertt exclaimed in horror. "Are you saying that he is retarded?"

"He doesn't have a disability," Mr. Evertt said flatly. "He is fine. He just needs a little time. He is young for his age."

"No, not retarded," Mrs. Rouch clarified calmly. "A learning disability. Specifically, he might have dyslexia. It is a very common condition. Tom Cruise and Cher both have dyslexia."

Mr. and Mrs. Evertt sat back in their chair in unison, obviously relieved and somewhat surprised. "Oh! That is much better. We were worried that you were going to put him in special education."

"Well," Mrs. Rouch paused slightly and smiled awkwardly. "First we need to do a formal evaluation, but . . . if the results confirm our suspicions, he might need to be placed in special education."

"I don't understand, isn't special education for kids with mental retardation?"

"No. In fact, most of our students in special education have average or above IQs. Some are even gifted academically."

"Then I don't understand. What is the difference between special education and regular education?" asked Mr. Evertt. "Back when we were younger, only kids with mental retardation went into special education and they had their own school building across town."

CASE STUDY QUESTIONS

After reading the case study and the rest of this chapter, you should be able to answer the following questions:

1. Is Mrs. Rouch correct about gifted students being served in special education programs?
2. Based upon his comments, where in the grief cycle is Mr. Evertt?
3. How has special education changed since the Evertts were in school?
4. What is the difference between special education and regular education?

INTRODUCTION

In order to help students who are in special education succeed in life we must first understand special education. In this chapter, we will be discussing several topics, including:

- The definition of special education
- The differences between regular and special education
- The history of special education
- Who is being served via special education programs
- The effects of being in special education on the student and their family

DEFINING SPECIAL EDUCATION

Despite its prevalence in public schools across the country, not many parents understand what special education is or how it is different from regular education. Many people erroneously believe that special education is for kids who have mental retardation or who are "stupid". This is certainly not the case! Perhaps the best place to begin is to define "special education" and then compare it to the education that most students receive.

In its simplest terms, special education is a federally mandated entitlement program that attempts to provide qualifying students with an appropriate individualized education. This definition certainly has many components. So let's break it down and discuss each in turn.

Federally Mandated

The foundation of special education is rooted in a series of pieces of federal legislation. Collectively, these laws require that states provide educational services to students with certain types of disabilities. While laws require services be provided, the courts, thorough their rulings on specific cases, help interpret these laws and determine how services should be furnished. The legal nature of special education is a complex one. Many texts are dedicated to explaining solely this topic (see Chapter 7 for additional resources). We will discuss the general legal nature of special education in Chapter 2.

Entitlement Program

So special education has to be provided in public schools because the federal government says that it has to. You are probably wondering, "Does that mean everybody can be enrolled in special education programs if they want to?" No. People who qualify for special education are entitled to it. That is, they cannot be turned away if they qualify.

Qualifying Students

So who qualifies for special education? Basically, in order to be entitled for special education, students must have a disability that adversely affects their education. Disabilities that could adversely affect education would include blindness, dyslexia, mental retardation, or oppositional defiant disorder. Disabilities that would not necessarily adversely affect education could include color blindness, amputees, and wheelchair users.

Appropriate and Individualize Education

As you can guess, there is more to qualifying for special education than simply having a disability that affects a student's learning. For example, suppose that you have a child who has a disability that adversely affects her education, such as dyslexia. Can she be denied special education services? Yes, especially if she is already receiving an "appropriate" education without any services at all. In other words, as we will talk about in chapter 2, special education is not supposed to give students the best education possible—just an "appropriate" education. So if your child with a learning disability is getting "A minuses" in all of her classes, but could be doing better if she had additional support, she might be denied special services because she is already achieving an "appropriate" education. What is an "appropriate" education? That is something that we will discuss when we talk about the legalities of special education later on in this book.

In addition to an appropriate education, special education guarantees that students with certain disabilities receive an individualized education. That is, they are given services based upon their individual needs. So, if your child needed help with her reading, she would be provided assistance based upon her specific difficulty.

THE DIFFERENCE BETWEEN SPECIAL EDUCATION AND REGULAR EDUCATION

There are several important factors that distinguish special education from regular education. You may wish to consider these differences prior to deciding if special education is appropriate for your child. Below several of these factors are discussed. Table 1.1 summarizes these discussions.

The Focus of Regular and Special Education

As we discussed earlier, special education is based upon the unique needs of individual students. Regular education, on the other hand, focuses upon the core content of the grade level or subject matter. A teacher in a first grade regular education class might teach her class how to add "2 + 2" even though some of her students might already have mastered this ability. In other words, the emphasis of regular education is not to address the needs of each student, but to move the class as a whole through the predetermined curriculum.

This is not to say that regular educators do not care about individual students. If a student is falling behind or requires extra help, regular educators often do what they can to get the student caught up. However, regular educators cannot jeopardize the progress of the entire class for the needs of one or two students.

This difference between special education and regular education is extremely important, especially when special education students are

Table 1.1. Special Education Versus Regular Education

	Special Education	Regular Education
Focus	Providing individualized instruction based upon the student's unique needs	Teaching a class of students from a predetermined curriculum
Educational Plans	Yes	No, with the exception of some gifted/talented or vocational programs
Parental and Student Input	Mandated by law	None required
Training	Emphasis on assessment, accommodations, teaching strategies, disabling conditions	Emphasis on subject or content area
Evaluation	Compliance to federal and state laws	Student achievement on standardized tests

included within regular education classes. Often a rift will develop between regular and special educators because they have different perspectives on the purpose of education. However, it is helpful to keep in mind that both professional care about their students. Each professional simply has a different focus.

Educational Plans and Parental Input

Another important difference between regular and special education involves the development of formal education plans. When a student enters special education—and at least every year thereafter—an educational plan is developed. We will discuss education plans in greater detail in Chapter 4; however, suffice to say that these plans are developed based upon the needs of the student with input from the student and his or her family members. In other words, parents of students in special education have considerable influence regarding what is taught to their child as well as how.

Suppose for a moment that you have a child without disabilities and you want his regular education teacher to teach a certain way. Perhaps you want the teacher to use more computer activities or group work. While a parent could certainly suggest to a regular educator that certain topics should be taught or specific strategies be used, a regular educator is not bound to change the curriculum based upon your input. In fact, a regular educator would be hard pressed to please all of his students' parents!

Now imagine that your child is in special education, but included within the regular educator's class. Can you make the regular educator change the way he teaches and use your suggestions? Yes—if your child's Individualized Education Plan (IEP) indicates that these strategies would help your child learn.

As we will talk later in greater detail, IEPs are legally binding contracts between the school and the parents that outline what services are going to be provided to students with disabilities. So if the IEP team decides that a student in special education needs more computer-based instruction in order to achieve an "appropriate" education, then the regular educator must comply. Through IEPs, therefore, parents have considerable influence on how and what educators teach.

The influence that parents of special education students have should not be taken lightly or abused. For instance, suppose that you are a regular educator who has several students with disabilities in your classes. Further, each of their parents wants something different! One set of parents wants you to utilize group activities. Another wants more one-on-one attention given to his or her child. Still another feels that you should be teaching social skills, rather than U.S. History. Even if you wanted to please everybody, you couldn't. Due to these types of experiences, many regular educators leave the teaching field all together!

The Training of Regular and Special Educators

Regular educators are trained much differently from their special educator peers. By and large, during their teacher preparation programs in college, regular educators are taught about specific subjects (e.g., social studies) or grade levels (e.g., elementary). They are trained to be masters of their content areas.

While special educators are given some information about content areas while in college, their training focuses primarily upon disabling conditions and methods for teaching diverse students. They are given skills to assess students' strengths and weaknesses. They are also able to develop strategies and accommodations that match a student's learning needs.

These professional differences can complement each other. However, in order to do so, regular and special educators must work together. Building a strong, collaborative relationship among regular educators, special educators, and parents is possibly the most important step in helping students with disabilities become successful in school. How to build effective collaborative teams will be discussed in Chapter 6.

The Evaluation of Regular and Special Educators

In addition to being prepared for their professions differently, regular and special educators are evaluated in substantially different ways. For example, regular educators are often judged by their students' scores on standardized and statewide assessments, such as the California Achievement Test (CAT) or Iowa Basics. If regular educators' students consistently score well below the school's overall average, school administrators might take a negative view of their teaching abilities. Consequently, such a teacher might be asked to leave the profession.

Special educators, on the other hand, are not evaluated based upon what their students have learned. Nor are they judged by whether or not their students ever achieve their IEP goals. Special educators are usually evaluated based upon the timeliness of their paperwork and whether they adhere to state and federal laws.

This is not to say that these are the only factors by which regular and special educators are judged. Clearly, if a special educator develops wonderful IEPs and is well informed regarding the latest court rulings and legislation, but does not teach or collaborate very well, school administrators are likely to be rather put out. School administrators also would probably be unhappy with regular educators who can teach well, but verbally abuse their students or colleagues. Still, the ways educators are evaluated are based largely upon the focus of their particular discipline.

THE HISTORY OF SPECIAL EDUCATION

There has never been a time when people with disabilities have not existed. Nor, barring major changes in medical science, will there ever be a day when people with disabilities cease to be. Still, understanding how special education developed, and has changed over recent years, may help your understand why special education is the way it is, as well as where it will be in the foreseeable future. In this section will briefly discuss the history of special education. Table 1.2 summarizes this discussion.

Prehistory

Recently, anthropologists uncovered the remains of a Neanderthal who had several life-altering infirmities. One of his arms was malformed, he would have been unable to walk, and he was probably blind in one eye. The interesting thing is that the skeleton was of an adult and many of these disabilities would have been present since birth. So, for many years, somebody had to have been taking care of this individual. This specimen suggests that caring for the disabled antedates the emergence of Homo sapiens.

The Birth of Special Education

Despite what Neanderthals might have done, most experts indicate that modern special education began with the work of Jean-Marc-Gaspard

Table 1.2.   A Brief History of Special Education

1799	Dr. Jean-Marc-Gaspard Itard begins working with Victor, the Wild Boy of Aveyron.
1817	Thomas Gallaudet opens the American Asylum for the Education of the Deaf and Dumb.
1832	Samuel Howe opens the New England Asylum for the Blind.
1876	Edouard Sequin founds the Association of Medical Officers of American Institutions for Idiots and Feebleminded Persons. It is later renamed to the American Association on Mental Retardation.
1878	Special education classes begin in Cleveland Public Schools
1905	Special education teachers begin to be trained.
1922	Council for Exceptional Children (CEC) is founded.
1949	The United Cerebral Palsy Organization is founded.
1950	The Association for Retarded Children, now called the ARC, is founded.
1954	Brown v. Board of Education court ruling ends separate but equal philosophy.
1963	The Association for Children with Learning Disabilities is founded.
1969	Swedish educator, Bengt Nirge, coins the term "normalization".
1972	Wolf Wolfensberger popularizes the term "normalization" in the United States. Pennsylvania Association for Retarded Children (PARC) v. Commonwealth of Pennsylvania ruling guarantees education to children with mental retardation. Mills v. Board of Education of the District of Columbia ruling guarantees right of education to all children with disabilities.
1973	Section 504 of the Rehabilitation Act is passed. It prevents discrimination based upon disability.
1974	The Education for all Handicapped Children Act, later renamed to the Individuals with Disabilities Education Act (IDEA), is passed.
1984	Rowley v. Hendrick Hudson School District ruling declares that schools must provide the services that students require to benefit from education.
1986	The reauthorization of IDEA mandates services for preschoolers with disabilities and requires that Individualized Family Service Plans be developed for each student receiving services.
1989	Timothy W. v. Rochester New Hampshire School District ruling reaffirms the right of even the most severely disabled students to get a free and appropriate public education.
1990	The Americans with Disabilities Act (ADA) passed. The reauthorization of IDEA mandates that transition be addressed for adolescents in special education.
1994	Gerstmyer v. Howard County Public Schools ruling awards damages to parents of a student with disability because the school did not conduct evaluations in a timely manner.
1997	IDEA is reauthorized.

Itard in the late 18th century. Itard worked with a boy named Victor who was found running wild in the woods of France. While Itard did not "cure" Victor or make him "normal", his work is recognized as the first systematic attempt to educate children with disabilities.

Special Education Comes to the United States

In 1848, Edouard Seguin, Itard's former student, immigrated to the United States, bringing with him many of Itard's ideas. Specifically,

Sequin advocated for the individualized instruction of children with cognitive disabilities. He also promoted the use of task analyses and gradually increased the complexity of tasks taught. His successes began to convince people that it is the responsibility of society to education children with disabilities. Thomas Gallaudet and Samuel Howe, educators of students with hearing and vision impairments, further championed this idea.

Two World Wars

The world wars of the 20th century affected the future of special education in two ways. First, with many able-bodied men away fighting, labor was in short supply. Consequently, women and people with disabilities were given unprecedented access to employment opportunities. Further, federal monies were used to train these newcomers to the workforce.

Secondly, the wars inundated the United States with disabled soldiers returning home from the front. Their sheer numbers brought the plight of individuals with disabilities to the forefront of the public's mind. Further, policymakers were well aware of the cost of caring for these soldiers for the rest of their lives. So legislation was passed to help them get back to work and live productive lives.

The Kennedy Era

Having had a sister with disabilities, President John F. Kennedy understood firsthand the needs of the disabled community. Before his death in 1963, Kennedy advocated for the causes of individuals with disabilities. In doing so, he moved the argument away from the economic issues raised by World War I and II and began focusing on the education of children with disabilities as a civil right. Students with disabilities, however, were still being served in schools other than those of their non-disabled peers. This soon would change.

The IDEA Becomes Clearer

Empowered by the Kennedy initiatives, the disabled community began to mobilize in ever-greater numbers during the 1970s. They became more politically active and helped pass numerous key pieces of legislation that guaranteed their access to education (such as what is now called the Individuals with Disabilities Education Act or IDEA). Further, the philosophy of physical and social inclusion began to drive the desire for students with disabilities to be educated with their non-disabled peers.

An Eye on the Future

As the 20th century came to a close, researchers began to learn that, although individuals with disabilities were now being given the opportunity to be included in regular education, few students experienced positive outcomes after leaving school. Specifically, after exiting high school, most adults with disabilities lived at home with their families and were unemployed. With this knowledge, a greater emphasis was placed upon preparing children with disabilities for their lives after school. Specifically, federal law mandated that adolescents begin addressing goals related to their movement from school to work.

The Doorstep of the 21st Century

* In the early history of special education, the education of children with disabilities was seen as a moral obligation. As time passed, the education of all children became a civil rights issue. At the present time, special education is based upon a moral and legal right that enables all children, regardless of the severity of their needs, to be educated with their peers. However, there is also an economic issue driving the preparation of students with disabilities for their future. Specifically, a great deal of emphasis is being placed on making sure students with disabilities will be able to work and support themselves.

In the future, it is likely that greater emphasis will be given to preparing children for their long-term and short-term, futures. For example, future legislation might mandate that all children and not just adolescents have plans in place that transition them from one part of their lives to another. Moreover, sexual education for students with cognitive disabilities is an area gaining interest as are issues related to early childhood.

Regardless of what happens in the future, one thing is certain. The special education of tomorrow will undoubtedly look much different than it does today. Parents of children with disabilities will have to keep informed and adapt to changes in laws and philosophies or else they will be unable to help prepare their children for their own changing world.

PEOPLE WITH DISABILITIES AND IN SPECIAL EDUCATION

When asked about special education most people seem to think of kids with profound mental retardation, sitting in wheelchairs, drooling on themselves. Occasionally, people might have heard about Down's syndrome, learning disabilities (such as dyslexia), or Attention Deficit Hyperactivity Disorder (ADHD). However, few people, even among regular educators understand the diversity that exists within the special education population.

People with Disabilities in General

Getting an accurate picture of how many people with disabilities live in the United States is rather problematic. First, there are many conflicting definitions of "disability". Second, there are many people who may qualify under various definitions, but do not regard themselves as disabled. As a result, they go uncounted. Further, there are many people who have been mislabeled with disabilities who should not be included in the overall total. Still, as a rough estimate, it is commonly believed that approximately 49 million Americans have disabilities that limit their functioning in some way (Wehman, Sherron, and West, 1997). This is slightly over 19 percent of the population of the United States. By way of comparison, there are more people with disabilities in the United States than African-Americans, who make up 12.3 percent of the United States' population (U.S. Census Bureau, 2000).

People in Special Education

Not everybody included within the 49 million have been served via special education. Nor do all of these people qualify for special education, as we will discuss later. At last count, there were over 5 million children enrolled in special education programs throughout the United States (U.S. Department of Education, 1999). As Table 1.3 indicates, the majority of these students have learning disabilities and only about 1 in 10 have mental retardation. This means that nearly 90 percent of students in special education have near-average or above-average

Table 1.3.   Students Served Via Special Education by Disability

Disability	Percent of Students in Special Education	Estimated Number
Learning Disabilities	51.0%	2,748,497
Speech or Language Impairments	19.8	1,065,074
Mental Retardation	11.2	602,111
Emotional Disturbed (Behavior Disorders)	8.4	454,363
Multiple Disabilities	2.0	106,758
Hearing Impairments	1.3	69,537
Orthopedic Impairments	1.2	67,422
Other Health Impairments	3.5	190,935
Visual Impairments	0.5	26,015
Autism	0.8	42,487
Traumatic Brain Injuries	0.2	11,895
Deaf-blindness	<0.01	1,454
Developmental Delay	<0.01	1,935
Total Students Served	~100%	5,388,483

Source: U.S. Department of Education (1999). *To Assure the Free Appropriate Public Education of All Children with Disabilities: Twenty-First Annual Report to Congress on the Implementation of the Individuals with Disabilities Act.* Washington, DC: U.S. Department of Education.

intelligence. In fact, many students in special education are actually gifted intellectually.

THE EFFECTS OF BEING IN SPECIAL EDUCATION ON STUDENTS AND THEIR FAMILIES

Deciding to enroll a child in special education may have many effects, both positive and negative, on the student as well as the family as a whole. Certainly one of the potential positives of special education programs is that students will begin to get the help that they need in order to succeed in school and life. Further, parents, through special education program, can be given the support and information that they may need to raise a child with special needs.

However, it cannot be denied that there may be less than positive outcomes of being enrolled in special education. First and foremost is the negative perception many people have regarding students who have disabilities, let alone those who are in special education. As we discussed earlier, many people think that students in special education are stupid. This simply isn't true. However, this perception can often permanently damage a student's self-esteem, especially if the student believes it.

Grief Cycle

Many theorists have equated having a child with disability to having a death in the family—which, for many people, might be fairly accurate. Think of it this way. When a couple finds out that they are going to have a child, they often fantasize about that child and the life he or she will have. They may picture the child growing up and becoming a doctor or famous athlete. They might dream of playing catch with their child on the front lawn or reading them stories as they fall asleep.

When a child is identified with a disability, many parents feel that these dreams have somehow ended. As a result, family members typically experience a series of powerful emotions after a child has been identified as having a disability. How family members address these emotions can affect not only their own lives, but also how they interact with their child.

Collectively, these emotions can be thought of in terms of a "grief cycle" (Kubler-Ross, 1969). They include feelings of:

- shock
- denial
- grief
- anger
- shame
- depression
- acceptance

Not everybody will learn to accept their situation. Nor will everybody progress through the stages in the same manner. Some people may never get over the shock of hearing that their child has a disability. Others may regress to later stages, such as anger. Below each of these stages is discussed, and potential strategies for helping family members cope with each stage are given. See Table 1.4 for a summary of the Grief Cycle.

Shock. Perhaps the first emotion that parents experience when their child is diagnosed with a disability is shock. They might feel as if their heart suddenly stopped or the wind got knocked out of them. Even if they suspected that something was "wrong" with their child, parents are often caught off guard when their child is labeled with a specific disability.

Table 1.4.   Summary of the Grief Cycle

Stage of Grief	Possible Strategies To Help
Shock	Give Time
Denial	Provide unbiased information
Guilt and Anger	Provide education
Shame and Depression	Provide support
Acceptance	Get them involved with the community

Family members who are within the shock stage of the grief cycle typically need time before they are able to move on. The amount of time they require will often depend upon the support that they have around them. So, during this stage, other family members and professionals should be supportive, rather than directive. Giving family members information about the disability or about program options might be overwhelming at this stage. Sometimes the best approach to helping family members who are in shock is to give them time to process what has just happened.

Denial.   After shock, family members may experience denial. They might claim that there is nothing wrong with the their child or insist that the difficulties that the child is having is normal. "He is just a slow learner," they might say.

Frequently, denial is rooted in a misunderstanding of what a disability is. Parents might think that a "learning disability" is just a politically correct term for "mental retardation" (which is not correct, as we will examine in Chapter 5). But you can't simply throw out facts and figures in order to persuade a family member that her child does in fact have a disability. When people are in denial, it is usually best to let them come to their own conclusions. They may need your guidance, but forcing them to "see the light" will not likely help them.

Providing family members in this stage with unbiased information might be the best approach. For example, rather than telling grandparents who do not believe that their grandchild has a disability that they are "wrong", you can explain what the disability is, assure them that the disability in and of itself is not bad, and then match the characteristics of the child to the disability.

Guilt and anger.   Many times parents will experience periods of profound guilt or anger. They may feel guilty that they didn't recognize the problem earlier or that they thought that the child wasn't trying in school. Imagine how you would feel if you spent a lot of time yelling at a child for not doing something only to learn that the child couldn't do it even if he or she wanted to.

Family members could also become angry. They might not be angry at anybody in particular. They might simply feel that life isn't fair or that they do not deserve to have this happening to them.

Support groups can often help family members overcome feelings of guilt and anger. They can talk to other people who experienced similar events and emotions. They can see that they are not alone or that there is hope. Providing family members with additional information might also help.

For instance, imagine a mother who thinks she caused her child's dyslexia because she had a glass of wine prior to learning that she was pregnant. She is likely to feel extremely guilty or angry at herself. She cannot come to accept what has happened until she first deals with her feelings. While a support group might be beneficial, educating the parent about the causes of dyslexia will help her understand that she did not cause her child's disability. Support and information are likely to help family members who are at this stage of the grief cycle.

Shame and depression. After feeling guilty or angry, family members might experience a sense of shame or depression. They might withdraw emotionally from others as they try to sort out what they are feeling. Perhaps for this reason, parents with children who have disabilities are more likely to get a divorce than other couples (Turnbull and Turnbull, 2001). Consequently, how families cope with these feelings is immensely important, not only to the welfare of children, but also to their family as a whole.

Support groups can also help family members who are depressed or feeling ashamed. So too can formal counseling. Group counseling with the entire family, and individual therapy, can be effective when used in tandem. Depressed family members could also do well by revisiting their faith and getting guidance from important figures in their lives, including religious leaders.

Acceptance. Acceptance comes when family members see their child as who they are—not a disabled or deviant child, but a child who just happens to have a disability. In fact, many times people will see conditions not as a disability, but a gift. For example, children with ADHD can be viewed as "hyperactive" or they can be viewed as potentially very productive. After all, who wouldn't want to have more energy? In that way, ADHD is something good to have.

Every cloud has a silver lining, although it is often difficult to see it during the storm. One way to get family members to see the positive in

Table 1.5.   Famous People with Disabilities

Albert Einstein (scientist)	Greg Louganis (athlete)
Galileo (scientist, inventor)	Winston Churchill (politician)
Mozart (composer)	Henry Ford (business person)
Wright Brothers (inventers)	Stephen Hawkings (scientist)
Leonardo da Vinci (artist, inventor)	Jules Verne (author)
Cher (singer)	Alexander Graham Bell (inventor)
Bruce Jenner (athlete)	Woodrow Wilson (politician)
Tom Cruise (actor)	Hans Christian Anderson (author)
Goya (painter)	Nelson Rockefeller (business person,
Charles Schwab (business person)	politician)
Henry Winkler (actor, director)	Thomas Edison (inventor)
Danny Glover (actor)	Gen. George Patton (general)
Milton (author, poet)	Agatha Christie (author)
F.D. Roosevelt (politician)	John F. Kennedy (politician)
Harriett Tubman (abolitionist)	Whoopi Goldberg (actor)
George Washington (general, politician)	Rodin (sculptor)
Walt Disney (business person)	Thomas Thoreau (author)
John Lennon (musician, artist)	David H. Murdock
Gen. Westmoreland (general)	Dustin Hoffman (actor)
Eddie Rickenbacker (race car driver,	Pete Rose (athlete)
fighter pilot)	Russell Varian
Harry Belafonte (actor, musician)	Robin Williams (actor, comedian)
F. Scott Fitzgerald (author)	Louis Pasteur (scientist)
Mariel Hemingway (actor)	Werner von Braun (scientist)
Steve McQueen (actor)	Dwight D. Eisenhower (general, politician)
George C. Scott (actor)	Robert Kennedy (politician)
Tom Smothers (actor, comedian)	Beethoven (composer)
Suzanne Somers (actor)	Carl Lewis (athlete)
Lindsay Wagner (actor)	"Magic" Johnson (athlete)
Napoleon Bonaparte (statesman)	Sylvester Stallone (actor)
Alexander the Great (statesman)	Prince Charles (British royalty)
Julius Caesar (statesman)	Vachel Lindsay (author)
Socrates (philosophers)	Truman Capote (author)
Vincent van Gogh (artist)	Peter the Great (statesman)
Peter Tchaikovsky (composer)	Michelangelo (artist)
Lord Byron (author)	George Bernard Shaw (playwright)
Edward Lear (author)	Pythagoras (philosopher)
Feodor Dostoevsky (author)	Georg Freidrich Handel (composer)
Gustave Flaubert (author)	Charles Dickens (author)

Source: http://laran.waisman.wisc.edu/fv/www/general/famous.html

their situation is to have them meet with other people who have already reached this stage. Further, having family members become active members of the community and help other parents of kids with disabilities may be rewarding in and of itself.

Another way for family members to come to see disabilities in a positive light is to educate them about famous people who have had disabilities (see Table 1.5). It is hard to view people with disabilities as stupid when you realize that Albert Einstein had a learning disability! So too did musician John Lennon and actor Tom Cruise. Learning to accept people with disabilities is often easier when we find out that people whom we already admire had disabilities themselves.

Many people feel that having child with a disability is a blessing. Facing such an adversity together often brings families together and makes them appreciate the things that they have. However, it is often a long road to get to this destination, and they may need help along the way.

Relationships within the Family

The manner in which family members adjust to having a disabled child will affect not only their own development, but the development of the entire family. For this reason, it is very important to focus attention on how the family is coping, not just the student with a disability. Below are some of the inter-family relationships and how having a child with special needs might affect them.

Marital relationships. Marital relationships are those between the child's parents—usually, but not always, the mother and father. These relationships are diverse, and change over time. For instance, when a couple first meets, they start out as strangers or acquaintances. As they get to know each other, they become friends, lovers, and then partners in life. When they have children, their relationship as friends, lovers, and partners typically becomes secondary to their roles as parents. Further, when their child has a disability, the child may require additional attention, thus taking more time away from the couple's marital relationships. The more severe the disability, the more likely it is that the child will need additional support, and thus more time.

When time is taken away from marital relationships, a great deal of stress can be put on the parents. As they spend less and less time together as friends or lovers, their other relationships might become weakened. Further, each parent might react to the disabling condition in different ways. They might progress through the grief cycle at different rates. For example, the mother might feel depressed while the father denies that there is a problem. In such circumstances, a couple would have a hard time supporting each other. The mother needs to be comforted, but the father may not see any need to be upset. Or perhaps they are at the same stage of grieving, but cope with their emotions differently. The mother might feel depressed and look to her spouse for strength, but the father may withdraw emotionally, maybe throwing himself into his work or extracurricular activities.

Certainly helping each parent through the grief cycle will help. Perhaps group counseling would also be beneficial. However, probably more than anything, parents need time to themselves. They need to be with each other as friends, lovers, and partners. Also, each parent needs time alone.

One way to help parents spend time together and by themselves is to give them the resources that they need. For instance, they might be able to use a list of babysitters who are skilled at working with special needs children. They may also need to be aware of support groups or sources of professional help. Even little things like knowing what restaurants are accommodating for people in wheelchairs could be beneficial. Much of this information can come from other parents. This is why getting parents to interact and support each other is so important.

By giving parents the resources that they need, their various marital relationships can be strengthened. The stronger these relationships, the more support will be in the family. The more support, the better off everybody will be.

Sibling relationships.   Within a family, siblings also have multiple relationships. They have relationships with each parent, which may differ over time and across genders. But they also have relationships with each other. When one child in the family has a disability, these relationships will undoubtedly be affected.

For example, if having a child with a disability takes time away from marital relationships, it also will take time away from the relationships between the parents and the child without a disability. These children might feel that they are not loved or do not get the attention that their sibling with a disability gets. They may grow to dislike or resent their sibling, thus diminishing the amount of support available for the family. Further, siblings are often required to act as care-providers for their disabled brother or sister. They may have to take care of them, putting a lot of stress on them. In essence, they might lose their childhood.

To help siblings, they should be encouraged to explore their own interests and be given time to themselves. They should also be given responsibilities that they can handle mentally as well as physically. They should also be able to spend time with their family regularly, aside from being a care-provider.

Extended family relationships.   Parents and siblings are not the only people who are affected when a child is identified with a disability. Extended family members, such as grandparents, may have difficulty adjusting as well. This is especially true if the grandparents do not understand the disability. They might be afraid or nervous when around the child because they do not know how to act. Further, grandparents could believe that the child's behavior is caused by poor parenting, and not a disability. This can cause great conflict between the grandparents and the child's parents, limiting the amount of support that the family gets during the time that they need it the most.

Even if grandparents understand their grandchild's disability and want to be supportive, they may have difficult performing activities typical of grandparents. For instance, elderly grandparents might not have the stamina to keep up with a hyperactive child. Or they may not have the strength to reposition a child in a wheelchair.

Like other family members, grandparents may need to be educated about their grandchild's condition. They may also need to be taught how to care for them, especially if the child requires special diets or physical regimens. Schools and professional organizations can provide the support that extended family members desire. Again, helping the entire family is the best way of helping the child.

Boxed Discussion 1.1:   Methods of Reducing Familial Stress

If not addressed, the stress of having a child with special needs can permanently damage a family. For example, there is a very high divorce rate among parents of children with disabilities. Further, siblings may end up taking on the roles of care providers before they are emotionally ready. For these reasons, it is very important to minimize the stress that families often feel. Below are several potential ways of reducing stress.

- Exercise regularly!
- Give each family member time for themselves.
- Communicate often. Perhaps have family meetings where everybody can voice their concerns or ideas.
- Develop interests not associated with special education or disabilities.
- Go out with friends on a regular basis.
- Get a massage.
- Soak in the bathtub.
- Keep a journal where you can vent privately.
- Talk to a counselor or supportive friend.
- Remember the good things.
- Keep things in perspective. Things probably aren't as bad as you think.

APPLYING WHAT YOU HAVE LEARNED

Go back and review the case study at the beginning of the chapter. Reflect on what has been covered in the chapter and try to answer the questions after the case study. What did you learn?

Question #1: Is Mrs. Rouch Correct About Gifted Students Being Served In Special Education Programs?

It is amazing how many people hear the words "special education" and think of kids with mental retardation or people in wheelchairs. This is not always the case. The majority of students in special education do not have mental retardation. But can a student be gifted and be in special education as Mrs. Rouch says?

Yes! People with super-high IQs can have disabilities too! For example, Stephan Hawkings, the famous physicist who writes about black holes, is extremely smart and he has several disabilities. He gets around by using a wheelchair, and he communicates through a computer. If he were in school now, he would be in special education. Please remember —SPECIAL EDUCATION DOES NOT MEAN STUPID!

Question #2: Based Upon His Comments, Where In The Grief Cycle Is Mr. Evertt?

Enrolling a child in special education affects not only the child, but his or her family members as well. As we discussed earlier, people have preconceived notions about special education and people with disabilities. For many family members, overcoming these erroneous notions takes considerable time and adjustment. Just look at how the Evertts responded in the case study. How are they dealing with the news that their child might have a disability?

Certainly the Evertts are both in shock. They apparently do not see anything "wrong" or "different" about their son, Michael. Mr. Evertt in particular seems to be having tough time accepting the fact that Michael might need to be enrolled in special education. In fact, he seems to be very much in the denial stages of the grief cycle that we talked about previously.

One way to help the Evertts adjust to their changing circumstances would be to educate them about disabilities and special education. Try to replace their misconceptions with the facts. Introduce them to people with disabilities, or tell them about famous people who have disabilities and have succeed in life. Also, give them time. Sometimes they just need to process what is happening.

Question #3: How Has Special Education Changed Since The Evertts Were In School?

In this chapter, we talked briefly about the history of special education and how it has changed dramatically over the years. Because of these changes, many people do not really understand what special education is or whom it serves. Many older people, such as the Evertts, still remember the days when special education pretty much served only kids with mental retardation or physical disabilities. Further, these students were placed in separate schools or separate classrooms.

Today, the majority of students in special education have average or above-average intelligence and are taught alongside their peers for at least part of the day. Further, with training and support, many students go on to college and live productive lives.

Question #4: What Is The Difference Between Special Education And Regular Education?

Since most students enrolled in special education are taught alongside their non-disabled peers, many parents might wonder what the difference is between regular and special education. This is actually a good question. In regular education, the focus is on the content for the entire class. In theory, everybody learns the same thing. Special education, on the other hand, focuses upon the unique needs of students who happen to have disabilities. What and how things are taught depends upon the individual's goals and objectives.

CHAPTER 2

The Legalities of Special Education

CHAPTER OBJECTIVES

Upon completing this chapter, you should be able to:

1. List the six main principles of IDEA.
2. Identify who is entitled to special education and who is not.
3. Define FAPE and LRE.
4. Discuss the "continuum of services" available to students in special education.
5. Outline the procedural due process.

CASE STUDY: THE LEGALITIES OF TEACHING ROLAND ROGAN

"In addition to the services that are currently spelled out in Roland's IEP," Mrs. Rogan continued after an already lengthy conversation with Roland's special education coordinator, Ms. Graff. "I would like Roland to receive a full-time aide to help him with his homework, an extra hour for each of his tests, and summer school to help him get ahead for next school year."

"Mrs. Rogan, these are all wonderful suggestions. And I am really pleased that you are taking such an active roll in your son's education, but . . ." Ms. Graff paused and smiled as politely as she could. "Roland is already getting mostly 'A's' in his courses. He is doing great with the amount of support that we are giving him now. He really doesn't need any additional assistance."

"Roland could be doing much better than he is. Yes, he is getting 'B's' and some 'A's', but he could be on the honor roll and be in accelerated courses. You yourself said that he could easily go to any college in the state. I just want him to get the best education possible."

"But he isn't entitled to the best education, just an appropriate one. He simply doesn't need any additional support from us. However, if you would like, I could recommend a very good tutorial program that he could use on his home computer."

"Would we have to pay for it?"

"Yes."

"Then let's put him in a self-contained classroom. At least there he will get the one-on-one attention that he deserves. He is just one of thirty students in the regular education classroom. He barely ever gets to speak with the teacher."

"A self-contained classroom wouldn't be appropriate for Roland," Ms. Graff insisted. "His IQ is too high. He would need to have mental retardation in order to be placed in a self-contained classroom, and as we have discussed, he has average intelligence. Because of his IQ, his LRE, or least restrictive environment, is in the general education classroom. If you disagree with these decisions, you can appeal them to the school principal."

CASE STUDY QUESTIONS

After reading the case study and the rest of this chapter, you should be able to answer the following questions:

1. Is Roland entitled to the services that his mother is requesting?
2. Is Ms. Graff correct about Roland's least restrictive environment?
3. Does Mrs. Rogan have to pay for the tutorial program?
4. If Mrs. Rogan disagrees with Ms. Graff, does she appeal the decisions to the school's principal?

INTRODUCTION

The legislation that governs special education is vast and complicated. If you want an exhaustive analysis of special education law and key court cases, please consult one of the many resources listed in Chapter 7. For the purposes of this text, a very general overview of the legal foundations that affect special education today will be described in this chapter. Topics we will be covering include:

- The Rationale Behind the Individuals With Disabilities Education Act (IDEA)

- The Six Main Principles of IDEA
- Other Legal Considerations

THE INDIVIDUALS WITH DISABILITIES ACT (IDEA)

It is impossible to talk about Special Education without discussing IDEA or the Individuals with Disabilities Education Act (Public Law 105-17). IDEA is the foundation upon which special education is built. As we discussed in the first chapter, IDEA has been revised several times. At the time of this book's publication, the latest reauthorization of IDEA occurred in 1997. You would do well to keep an eye open for future authorizations. The laws that guide the special education process change frequently. Joining professional organizations, such as the Council for Exceptional Children (CEC) and The Association for Persons with Severe Handicaps (TASH) is one way to keep current on special education law.

THE RATIONALE BEHIND IDEA

Perhaps, the first question that you have is, "why do we need laws like IDEA?" According to lawmakers, the rationale behind IDEA is to:

Assure that all children with disabilities have available to them . . . a free appropriate public education . . . designed to meet their unique needs, to assure that the rights of children with disabilities and their parents or guardians are protected, to assist states and localities to provide for the education of all children with disabilities, and to assess and assure the effectiveness of efforts to educate children with disabilities (IDEA, 20 U.S.C. 1400[c]).

But more simply stated, laws like IDEA outline the bare minimum of services that society provides to its citizens. Without laws, the civil liberties of all people, not just those with disabilities can be infringed upon.

THE SIX MAIN PRINCIPLES OF IDEA

IDEA is comprised of six interrelated principles that set the guidelines for how special education is provided to students with disabilities. None of these principles is absolute. Court rulings have helped differentiate what these principles mean. Each is discussed below and summarized in Table 2.1.

Table 2.1.   Summary of IDEA'S Six Main Principles

Principle	Summary
Zero Reject	Students who qualify for special education cannot be denied services
Nondiscriminatory Identification and Evaluation	Assessments must be multifaceted and protect against bias
Free and Appropriate Public Education (FAPE)	Students are guaranteed an "appropriate" education at no cost to the parents, not the "best" education possible.
Least Restrictive Environment (LRE)	Students with disabilities must be educated along side of their nondisabled peers as much as possible.
Parental and Student Participation	Parents and students must be given opportunities to participate in the IEP process.
Procedural Due Process	Parents and school officials have the right to settle conflicts through neutral third parties.

- Zero Reject
- Nondiscriminatory Identification and Evaluation
- Free and Appropriate Public Education (FAPE)
- Least Restrictive Environment (LRE)
- Parental and Student Participation
- Procedural Due Process

Zero Reject

As we discussed briefly in Chapter 1, students who qualify for special education services cannot be turned away. But who qualifies for special education? This is a bit tricky. Consider the following.

Age. If a child between the ages of 6 and 17 has a disability that adversely affects their ability to gain an "appropriate" public education, they are entitled to special education services. Further, if the state provides educational programs to non-disabled children between the ages of 3 and 5 or 18 and 21, the state must also provide special education services to children with disabilities of the same ages. So, if a state provides education to students without disabilities from age 3 to 21, they must also provide services to students with disabilities of the same age.

Severity of disabilities. You might be asking yourself, "What if a child has profound and multiple disabilities? Does the state have to provide special education services?" The answer is "yes."

Many people still hold the view that certain students are "uneducable." That is, some students are "too disabled" to learn. These people may state that IDEA does not guarantee special education if the student would not benefit from services. However, this is clearly not true and is illustrated in the famous court case Timothy W. v. Rochester School District.

Timothy W. was a thirteen-year-old student who was deaf and blind. He also had cerebral palsy, experienced numerous seizures, and was labeled as profoundly mentally retarded. His school district refused to provide services to Timothy because school officials felt that he would not benefit from them. The court ruled in favor of Timothy's parents saying that IDEA intends to provide education to all students regardless of their functioning-level or prospects for success.

Contagious diseases and conditions.   Now you are probably thinking, "What if a student has some sort of disease that is contagious and can infect other students? Is the student still guaranteed a free and appropriate public education?" The answer is still "yes", but with qualifications.

Suppose that Timothy was deaf and blind as well as afflicted with a disease that could be spread to other students, such as AIDS or tuberculosis. IDEA still mandates that he would be eligible for a free and appropriate public education. However, this does not mean that all students in this situation have to receive their education with other students.

If Timothy had a condition that constituted a significant health risk to other people, he could have been educated at his home or in a hospital. Further, the state would still have to pay for the services he receives.

Who determines whether a student poses a significant risk to other students or teachers? Most of the time, the IEP (Individualize Education Plan) team determines where a student will be educated. (We will discuss this when we get to Least Restrictive Environment.) However, when a student has a contagious condition, the IEP team typically turns to medical authorities to determine the appropriate placement. In such cases, a panel of medical doctors usually examines all of the available evidence and makes a recommendation. In many cases, such as with Ryan White (Ryan White was a child with AIDS who was discriminated against by his peers and school) and other victims of AIDS, the school is still a safe environment if the appropriate precautions are taken.

Violent students.   Suppose now that Timothy does not have a contagious disease, but is still a threat to his peers and teachers. Perhaps, his behavior is so violent that he is likely to hurt somebody. Could he be denied special education then?

If Timothy were violent, the situation would be very similar to if he had a contagious disease. He would still be entitled to special education, but he could be taught someplace other than the regular education classroom, such as a lock-down juvenile detention facility. Again, he could not be denied special education just because of his behavior.

Expulsions and suspensions.   Another question that you may have is "Can a student in special education be expelled or suspended?" Unfortunately, the answer to this is a bit convoluted and people are often misinformed.

Let's suppose the Timothy qualifies for special education. Let's further suppose that one of his disabilities is a conduct disorder, which is characterized by inappropriate, and often hostile, behavior. (Conduct Disorder will be discussed and defined in Chapter 5). If Timothy did something that would normally get a non-disabled student expelled or suspended, he may or may not receive the same punishment.

In an important case (Honig v. Doe), a student with mental retardation was expelled for putting alcohol in the punch at a school dance. The Supreme Court ruled that the student could not be expelled or suspended since the behavior in question was the result of his disability (i.e., the student didn't know what he was doing was wrong due to his mental retardation). So does this mean that a student in special education cannot be punished? After all, few behaviors would not involve a student's mental retardation. The answer to this question is unclear.

Recent court rulings have clouded the issues related to expelling or suspending students. School officials are now allowed to temporarily remove dangerous students from their placement until it can be determined whether the student should be placed in a different environment. So if Timothy brought a gun to school and started shooting at his peers, the school's officials could remove Timothy from school even though his behavior was due to his cognitive disability. However, they can only remove Timothy for 45 days. After that, they have to return him to his prior classroom or, if the IEP team agrees, to a better placement.

It should be noted that, in some cases, punishing a student in special education just like any other student might be advantageous. For example, if Timothy thought that he could do whatever he wanted "because he has a disability", he may not develop the social skills that he needs in order to succeed in life. Therefore, his parents might like to have their son experience consequences from his actions. In these cases, the IEP could be amended so that when Timothy did something wrong, an already agreed upon plan of action would be followed. Further, Timothy might have a behavioral contract that outlines what is expected of him and what would happen if he disregards school rules.

Nondiscriminatory Identification and Evaluation

The second key principle of IDEA involves the identification and evaluation of students. Specifically, IDEA attempts to guard against over-identification of minority populations for special education services. It does so by requiring that the assessment process be multifaceted. That is, a wide array of assessment tools and evaluators should be used to determine whether a student is eligible for special education. No decision should be made based upon the information provided by a single test or assessor. Moreover, the assessments must be given in the student's native language. So if a student speaks Norwegian, the school must find an interpreter who also speaks Norwegian.

Free and Appropriate Public Education

The primary goal of special education is to provide a free and appropriate public education. This is sometime referred to as FAPE. There are three key concepts within FAPE:

- Free
- Appropriate
- Public

Free.   IDEA mandates that the education students with disabilities receive should be without cost to the student's family. Special education services are financed through a combination of state, local, and federal funds. However, the issue is not as cut and dried as it seems.

Suppose that parents want an expensive computerized communication device for their child with autism. Does the school have to pay it? It depends.

If the student is already communicating fine without the device or there is a better, less expensive option—then no, the school does not have to pay. However, if the student is not currently receiving an "appropriate" education and the device will help reach that end—then yes, the school has to pay for it.

Appropriate.   As we mentioned in Chapter 1, students with disabilities are not guaranteed the best education possible. They are simply
guaranteed access to a free and appropriate public education or (FAPE).
But what exactly does "appropriate" mean?

In a landmark court case (Board of Education of the Hendrick Hudson
Central School District v. Rowley), parents wanted a school to pay for an
interpreter for their daughter who had a significant hearing loss. The parents felt that the interpreter would help their child achieve her full potential, just as students without disabilities are able to do. The school argued
that the student didn't need any additional assistance because she was an
excellent lip-reader and was doing well in school without the interpreter.

The case made it all the way to the United States Supreme Court. In
a split decision, the court ruled that schools need not be concerned with
maximizing a student's potential. Rather, an "appropriate" education
involves enough support so that the student benefits educationally from
attending school. According to the courts' interpretation of IDEA, an
appropriate education does not exist when the student is not making
progress, is making only minimal progress, or is actually regressing.
This is called the benefit standard.

Public.   Another important word within FAPE is "public." However,
this does not mean that all students in special education have to go to
public school. As we will discuss next, special education services can be
provided in many diverse environments, including private institutions.

Least Restrictive Environment

Perhaps the most important, and misunderstood, principle of IDEA is
its mandate for a Least Restrictive Environment, or LRE. IDEA orders
that children in special education be taught alongside of their non-
disabled peers as much as possible. However, despite what some people
believe, this does not mean that all students with disabilities are entitled
to be taught in the regular classroom at all times.

Imagine a student in special education who is very violent. He kicks
and bites anybody who gets near him. Maybe he even threatens to kill
his fellow students. Where is his least restrictive environment? Well, it
really depends. He might be able to do the work in the regular classroom. In fact, he might be gifted and could be in advanced courses. But,
because of his behaviors, a self-contained classroom might be the most
appropriate placement for him.

Now, imagine a student with profound mental retardation, autism, and hearing impairments. Clearly she needs intensive support in order to master rudimentary skills. Maybe she even needs some assistance to go to the bathroom. Where is her least restrictive environment? Again, this depends. This student's IEP team may feel that she should be included within the regular classroom, simply so she can socialize with her non-disabled peers.

LRE is based upon each student's individualized needs. It is not based upon IQ or number of disabilities or any formula. Nor is every student entitled to be fully included in the regular education classroom. However, under IDEA, every student is guaranteed a placement as least restrictive as possible.

So, what placements options are available to students and how do IEP teams determine which is the best for the student? Below is a brief discussion of some of the possible environments in which students with disabilities might be placed (see Table 2.2 and Figure 2.1). They include:

- Special Non-Academic Facilities
- Special Academic Facilities
- Separate Classrooms
- Resource Rooms
- Regular Classrooms With Support From Special Education
- Regular Classrooms With Support From Regular Education
- Regular Classrooms Without Any Special Support

Special non-academic facilities. Special non-academic facilities are placement options that focus on skills other than academics and are

Table 2.2.   Examples of Possible LRE Placements

Possible LRE	Examples
Special Non-Academic Facilities	Prison, Chemical Treatment Facility, Hospital
Special Academic Facilities	Home School, School for the Deaf, School for the Cognitively Gifted, School for the Performing Arts
Separate Classrooms	Self-Contained Classroom
Resource Rooms	Reading Resource Room, Tutor Rooms
Regular Classrooms With Support From Special Education	Regular education room with assistance from special education aid or interpreter
Regular Classrooms With Support From Regular Education	Regular education room with modifications to tests or instruction
Regular Classrooms Without Any Special Support	Same services given to all regular education students

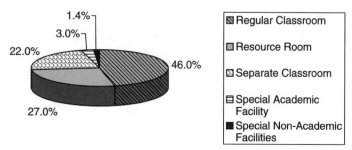

Figure 2.1.   *Percent of Student Served in Various LREs*

Source: U.S. Department of Education (1999). *Twenty-First Annual Report to Congress on the Implementation of the Individuals with Disabilities Education Act.* Washington, DC: U.S. Government Printing Office.

not associated with a school. For example, they could include lock-down detention facilities, in-patient treatment centers, or residential programs. Students might be placed in a special non-academic facility because they are violent, a physical risk to themselves, or medically fragile. Students who are attempting to kick their drug or alcohol habits might be sent to a rehabilitation center, which is an example of this type of placement.

Special academic facility.   Special academic facilities are environments that focus upon the academic needs of students but are not part of the regular schools to which most students go. Examples include schools for the deaf or hearing impaired and schools for children who are autistic or profoundly mentally retarded. Home schools and special schools for the cognitively gifted can also be considered part of these options.

Separate classroom.   Another LRE placement in which students in special education can find themselves involves separate classrooms from their non-disabled peers. These environments are within the same school that non-disabled students attend, but they are not connected directly with the regular classrooms. For example, there might be a hallway where all of the specialized classes are located.

Resource room.   Many times students with disabilities are placed in multiple environments. They might be included within the regular classroom for part of their time and then receive specialized services in a resource room for the rest of the day. For example, a student with dyslexia might need assistance only with reading. So, during the reading portion of the general education curriculum, the student will go to a resource room where a special education teacher or aid helps the student. During the rest of the day, the student would remain with his or her peers. This is an example of what is often called a pullout program.

The amount of time a student spends in resource or regular education classrooms can vary based upon the student's needs. A student might spend only a few minutes a week in a resource room, such as when a test is being given. Or students may spend all of their time in a resource room, with the exception of when certain subjects are covered in the regular classroom, such as math or art. Again, the degree to which a student is included within the regular classroom depends only upon the student's needs, not his or her disability or IQ.

Regular classroom with support from special education. For many students with disabilities, the regular classroom might be the best environment for their specific needs. However, in order to succeed in the regular classroom, they might need a little extra help from the special education department. For example, they might need an aide helping them to stay on task or they may need a sign language interpreter. In such cases, the student's LRE would be the regular classroom with supports. The difference between this placement and the previous one is that, for this placement option, all services are provided within the regular classroom, whereas some supports in the previous options are presented elsewhere (e.g., resource rooms).

Regular classroom with support from regular education. Not all students need support from special education. For example, suppose that a student with ADHD has problems paying attention during class lectures. Rather than having an aide from special education sit with him and keep him on task, the student could be given lecture notes from the regular education teacher. The notes would help the student follow along and focus upon the important details. This type of support is based upon the unique needs of the student, but is not provided by any of the special education staff.

Regular classroom without any special support. The next placement option available to students with disabilities is obviously in the regular classroom but without any special supports. That is, the student with disabilities is treated exactly the same as any other student receiving a regular education. The teacher may not even know that the student has a disability.

Technically, students who can successfully receive an appropriate education in regular education without support are probably not eligible for special education. However, many students who receive special education services will eventually not need them. In other words, being enrolled in special education is not a life sentence. If the correct services are provided, a student with disabilities can eventually return to the regular classroom as a traditional student. Remember, one of the unstated goals of special education is to give students with disabilities the skills that they need to succeed in life, which includes the regular education classroom. So every service provided to students should help move them back to the regular classroom.

Determining a student's LRE.   Many people portray the placement options available to students as a continuum. That is, being fully included in the regular education classroom is seen as being less restrictive than getting services in a hospital or juvenile detention center. The premise underlying this viewpoint is that one option is somehow better than another—that being fully included in the regular classroom is the best placement option. This view is counterproductive and could actually be harmful to student.

Rather than seeing placement options as a continuum with good or bad endpoints, view them as tools that can help students achieve their goals. Certainly every child with a disability could be placed full-time in the regular education classroom. But not every child would benefit from this environment. The same is true with being placed in a resource room or special non-academic setting as well. In fact, many students who are misplaced may lose ground and fail to achieve an appropriate public education. So how do you determine where each student should be taught?

There is no clear formula or guidelines that dictate how and where students with disabilities should be served. However, in their ruling for the Board of Education, Sacramento City Unified School District v. Holland, a federal court outlined two broad factors that must be taken into consideration when determining a student's LRE:

- the benefit to the student, and
- the effects on other students or faculty.

Benefit to the student.   Clearly, one of the principal concerns of IDEA is the education of students with disabilities. So, the environment in which services are provided should benefit the student. It should be noted that not all benefits need be academic. For example, a student might benefit socially from his or her placement. The key is that if an environment does not benefit a student, then it is not that student's LRE.

The same is true if the environment's negatives outweigh its positives. In other words, if a student would learn social skills in a regular classroom, but not academic skills, the IEP team might decide that the student's LRE is in the resource room for part of the day.

Let us suppose that a student with a very mild learning disability could do just fine within the classroom with a few modifications and supports, such as extra time taking spelling tests. But the IEP team wants to put the student in a self-contained classroom especially for kids with similar disorders. Their argument is that the more one-on-one attention that the student receives, the better he will do. Where is this student's LRE?

Remember that the LRE stands for "Least Restrictive Environment," not the "Environment where the Student would Learn Best." According to IDEA, students should be removed from regular education only to the extent necessary needed to provide a FAPE. So students should not be placed in the environment where they learn the most, but in the environment in which they can get an appropriate education with the least amount of supports necessary. In the case described above, the student should be placed in the regular classroom with minimal supports—not a self-contained classroom with more supports than he needs, even if those supports would be beneficial.

. *Effects on other students and faculty.*   The right to special education does not override the rights of non-disabled students or their teachers. Remember the student that we discussed earlier, the one who was very violent? That student might learn more in the regular classroom than in any other environment; however, he is a danger to the rest of the class. In such cases, a student's LRE could be a separate classroom or school.

Weighing the interests of the student versus the rest of the class is not always cut and dried. This is especially true when the regular education teacher clearly does not want to have students with any type of disability. In the end, the IEP Team has to decide whether the needs of the special education student supersede the effects on the regular educator and the non-disabled students. Table 2.3 outlines some areas to consider when determining a student's LRE.

Parental and Student Participation

The fifth component of IDEA involves parental and student participation. This means that the law allows parents and student to be integral

Table 2.3.   Areas to Consider Prior to Determining LRE

• Intensity of supports needed by student	• Long-term goals
• Academic needs	• Duration of services needed
• Social needs	• Values of the family
• Availability of accommodations	• Safety of the student and peers
• Training of educators	• Preferences of the student

parts of the IEP and assessment processes. Parents and, when possible, the student are key members of the IEP team that helps determine what services are provided and what goals are addressed. Their input must be actively sought and incorporated into the decision-making process.

It should be noted that parents need not be biologically related to the student, in order to be allowed to participate. The right to participate in the decision-making process is granted to all legal guardians of the student. Further, if parents, or legal guardians, want additional people to participate in the decision-making process (e.g., grandparents, friends, or advocates), they have a right to invite them to all meetings.

Procedural Due Process

Finally, IDEA guarantees procedural due process when conflicts arise between the school and parents. This component not only protects you and your child, but the school as well.

Suppose for a moment that you have a student with mental retardation whom you want to be placed 100 percent of the time in the regular education classroom with a full-time aide. The school disagrees and thinks that your child should be placed in a resource room for the entire day with the exception of physical education, art, and music. How do you determine who is right?

Procedural due process is a multifaceted mechanism. As soon as your child enters special education, you must be notified of your rights. This notification must be in writing and in a manner that you can understand. Further, this notification must be given to you at least every year.

If parents and the school cannot agree, they can go to mediation. Basically, the parents and school officials meet and attempt to work out their differences. There might even be an uninvolved third party who guides the conversation.

If, after trying to work out their differences, the parents and school officials still do not see eye-to-eye, a due process hearing is held. A due

process hearing is much like a mini-trial. Both sides present information, call and cross-examine witnesses, and attempt to show why their
position is in the best interest of the student and within the guidelines
outlined by IDEA. An uninvolved third party, called the due process
hearing officer, weighs the arguments and makes a decision based upon
the information provided.

What if either party does not like the decision of the due process
hearing officer? In such cases, parents or school officials can appeal the
decision to a state or federal court. As with any legal matter, decisions
of lower courts can be appealed to higher courts. In the end, the highest
court (i.e., the United States Supreme Court) would have the final say.

OTHER LEGAL CONSIDERATIONS

The six components of IDEA are not the only legal implications of having a child in special education programs. There are many more legalities, far more than can be discussed in this chapter. Below are a few extra
legal issues about which you might have questions. If you need more
legal guidance, you may want to consult some of the resources presented
in Chapter 7 or meet with a lawyer specializing in disability law.

Access to All Information

In addition to all of the rights guaranteed by IDEA outlined above,
federal law also gives parents access to all information regarding their
child. This means that any information regarding your child must be
given to you upon your request. This includes any formal or informal
assessments as well as notes that teachers make on your child's
progress. It even means that you have a right to see a teacher's personal
journal if the teacher writes about your child.

Confidentiality

Another legal aspect of special education involves confidentiality. Information regarding your child should be classified. The only people
who have access to this information are members of the IEP Team. Even
regular educators who have special education students in their classrooms can be prevented from looking at their students' files. Further,
schools cannot publish lists of students who receive special educational

services. Nor can they make public the IEPs of students without the consent of the student's parents.

Informed Consent

Not only do parents have to be informed prior to any changes to a student's formal educational program, but they also must give their consent to these changes. This means that school personnel need to provide you with a rationale for, as well as potential positives and negatives of, the proposed changes. Does this mean that parents need to know about and agree to everything that goes on within their child's classroom? No.

Teachers need only inform and gain the consent of parents to matters that affect the student's IEP. For example, teachers must gain informed consent if they want to change the student's LRE or if they want to reassess the student for a disability. They do not have to contact parents if they want to show a video instead of lecture, or postpone a spelling quiz.

Suppose that a teacher wants to use time-out strategies as a way of disciplining a student. Does the teacher have to get the consent of the student's parents? It depends.

If the IEP specifies how the student is to be disciplined and the teacher wants to change it, then the teacher must inform the parents and gain their consent. If the IEP does not indicate how the student will be disciplined, then the teacher can use the time-out procedures. Even if this second scenario is the case, it is a matter of common courtesy that the teacher keep in touch with the student's parents and inform them of what is transpiring in the classroom.

Re-evaluations

In the past, we talked about Zero Reject. Basically, that means that a student who is eligible for special education cannot be denied access to special education services. However, this does not mean that once in special education, always in special education. In fact, many students benefit so much from special education services that they no longer need them. This is particularly true for students with emotional or behavioral problems who learn the skills they require to succeed in the general education classroom.

Because students might "outgrow" special education, it is important to frequently re-evaluate students to see if they still have a disability that adversely affects their ability to obtain a free and appropriate public education. According to federal law, this must be done at least every three years. However, the re-evaluation process should be an ongoing one. So, every year when you are updating your child's IEP, the IEP Team should address whether services are still needed.

Attorney Fees

Sometimes, when conflicts cannot be settled any other way, parents will have to hire lawyers to represent them at due process and legal proceedings. When this occurs, the school might have to pay for the parent's legal fees. Under the Handicapped Children's Protection Act of 1986 (HCPA), parents can be awarded reasonable attorney fees if they prevail in their case. It is up to the courts to determine what "reasonable" is and whether parents should recoup any of what they paid.

Unachieved IEP Goals and Objectives

IEPs are legally binding contracts between the school and the student's parents. So you might be wondering what would happen if annual goals are not achieved? Can you sue the school?

Boxed Discussion 2.1:   The Rights of Parents of Students in Special Education

There are many rights that come with having a child who has special needs. Below are some of the rights that IDEA guarantees parents (i.e., legal guardians):

- You must give your consent to have your child tested and enrolled in special education.
- You must be notified of any changes in placement.
- You must be given the full results of evaluations.
- Information must be furnished in such a way so you understand it, even if this means getting an interpreter or having materials written in your native language.
- You have the right to see what records are kept on your child.
- You can remove from your child's file any records that you feel are misleading or inaccurate.
- You have a right to confidentiality. Only members of the IEP team can have access to your child's records. Other people must have your written consent.
- Your child must be taught in the least restrictive environment possible.
- You have the right to participate in the development of your child's educational plans. This means that the meetings have to be schedule at a time and place that is conducive to your schedule.
- You can invite anybody you like to your child's IEP meeting.
- You have the right to appeal any decision made about your child.

In most cases you could not sue the school simply because your child did not achieve the goals and objectives written into an IEP. After all, it is probably not the school's fault if a student does not accomplish the desired outcome. Maybe the goal or objective was too hard or the student did not try.

However, suppose that a school did not do anything to help a student achieve his or her goals or objectives. For instance, instead of teaching the student, the teachers had him sit quietly at his desk all day, every day. According to the law, schools must make a good faith effort to teach students. If a school does not do this, then parents can sue.

APPLYING WHAT YOU HAVE LEARNED

Go back and review the case study at the beginning of the chapter. Reflect on what has been covered in the chapter and try to answer the questions after the case study. What did you learn?

Question #1: Is Roland Entitled To The Services That His Mother Is Requesting?

Roland's mother is asking for many potentially useful services. She is clearly trying to give her son a leg-up on his future. The question is— is Roland entitled to these services? What do you think?

At the very heart of special education is the idea of FAPE, or Free and Appropriate Public Education. As Ms. Graff indicated in the case study at the beginning of the chapter, students in special education are not entitled to the best education possible, just an "appropriate" education. Defining "appropriate", however, is rather problematic. Everybody has a different definition.

Certainly it can be argued that Roland is already getting an "appropriate" education since he is presently getting "B's" and "A's". But there are no set guidelines. Are all "C's" indicative of an appropriate education? What about all "D's"? What constitutes an appropriate education is often decided by a due process hearing officer.

Question #2: Is Ms. Graff Correct About Roland's Least Restrictive Environment?

Another important component of special education is least restrictive environment, or LRE. As we discussed earlier in this chapter, IDEA mandates that every student in special education be taught in their LRE. Ms. Graff seems to think that Roland's LRE is in the general education classroom. Is this correct?

This is a difficult question that cannot be correctly answered based upon the information provided in the case study. A student's LRE is not based upon a student's IQ, as Ms. Graff incorrectly states. A student's LRE is based upon the student's unique needs. So, if Roland had severe behavior problems and was a threat to himself or others, his least restrictive environment might be in a self-contained classroom or even in an institution. In other words, while IDEA insists that the IEP team justify why a child is not placed with his or her peers, it does not say that all children should be placed in the regular education classroom.

Question #3: Does Mrs. Rogan Have To Pay For The Tutorial?

Students in special education are guaranteed a free appropriate public education (FAPE). Does this mean that Mrs. Rogan has to pay for the tutor that she wants? What do you think?

The "free" part of FAPE is not exactly cut and dried. If a student, such as Roland, is already getting an appropriate education, then yes, his family has to pay for the tutor. If, on the other hand, Roland needed a tutor in order to achieve an appropriate education, then the school would most likely have to pay for it.

Question #4: If Mrs. Rogan Disagrees With Ms. Graff, Does She Appeal The Decisions To The School's Principal?

In many IEP meetings, there are disagreements between team members. Perhaps parents want their child to have an expensive communication device that the school administrator doesn't want to have to buy. Or maybe the regular educator thinks that the student should be placed in a resource room whereas everybody else things full inclusion within the general classroom is more appropriate. These disagreements are common and understandable. Each team member has a different perspective and philosophy. But what happens when team members just can't come to an agreement, such as Mrs. Rogan and Ms. Graff?

If team members simply cannot resolve their differences, the first step is to have a third party who is not involved mediate the conflict. If the mediation does not work, the team members can meet with a due process hearing officer. The hearing officer then hears both sides, evaluates the evidence, and then makes a ruling. Despite what Ms. Graff indicated, Mrs. Rogan does not formally appeal decisions to the principal, although Mrs. Rogan certainly can bring up her concerns to the school's administration, if she wishes.

CHAPTER 3

The Special Education Process

CHAPTER OBJECTIVES

Upon completing this chapter, you should be able to:

1. List the steps involved in the special education process.
2. Identify what happens before a student is referred to special education.
3. Identify what happens after a student is enrolled in special education.
4. Describe what is involved in a nondiscriminatory evaluation.
5. Explain when IEPs are reevaluated.
6. List and contrast different types of formal plans individuals with disabilities might have.

CASE STUDY: THE PROBLEMS OF J.R. REILLY

· "Dr. Johansen?" Mrs. Reilly asked as she gripped the phone a little tighter than she normally would. "This is Sarah Reilly, J.R.'s mother. Do you have a moment?"

"Yes, of course. What can I do for you?"

"Well, it is about J.R." Mrs. Reilly continued. "He still isn't doing very well in school. He can't seem to sit still and he never pays attention to me when I am talking to him. He has so much energy . . . " Mrs. Reilly paused for a moment to collect herself. "I think he has that ADHD. I talked to his pediatrician and she agrees."

"I understand," Dr. Johansen said reassuringly. She had been the principal of the elementary school that J.R. attended for many years and she had learned to tell when a parent needed a little extra support. "That isn't a problem in and of itself. In fact, there are many famous and successful people who have Attention Deficit Hyperactivity Disorder, such as actor Robin Williams. I just read a book on how ADHD can actually be a gift, if the students can be taught on how to utilize their energy in positive ways. It's called Teaching Superman How To Fly."

"Well, that is just it. He is certainly a bright kid. And very creative. But he needs a little extra help. Is there anything that we can do to give him the help that he needs so he doesn't fall further behind in school?"

"Yes, indeed. We have a wonderful teacher in our special education program who is an expert in these matters. He really understands these kids and helps them learn the skills that they will need to succeed later in life."

"Special ed?" Mrs. Reilly said doubtfully.

"I know what you are thinking," Dr. Johansen said with a slight laugh. "Special education is often misunderstood. It isn't just for kids with mental retardation or cerebral palsy. It helps a lot of students who just need a little extra assistance. Why, we even have some students who are gifted in special education. Special education doesn't mean 'stupid' it just means 'additional help'. In fact, most people will not even know that J.R. is in special education. He will be taught in the same classroom as he is in now, but he will probably go into a resource room a couple times a week to get extra tutoring."

"I suppose that would be fine. What do I need to do? Does he need to have some sort of formal evaluation or anything?"

"It sounds like you have already done it. Send me name of your pediatrician and we will set up a meeting to enroll J.R. in our special education program. You and I will meet with the special education teacher and go over all the paperwork and develop what is called an IEP or Individualized Education Plan. This outlines J.R.'s goals and how we will try to help him. Every few years, we will reexamine where he is and rewrite the IEP to suit his changing needs."

"Okay," Mrs. Reilly said faintly. "I will send you the information and schedule a meeting for us to develop the IEP-thing."

CASE STUDY QUESTIONS

After reading the case study and the rest of this chapter, you should be able to answer the following questions:

1. Was the special education process followed in J.R.'s case study?
2. Did J.R. receive a nondiscriminatory evaluation?

3. When should J.R.'s IEP be re-evaluated?
4. Other than an IEP, what other kinds of formal plans might J.R. have?

INTRODUCTION

The purpose of this chapter is to delineate the step-by-step process that special education follows. Generally, the special education process follows eight steps. Each of these is discussed below. Figure 3.1 outlines this process in a flow chart.

- Identification of a Problem
- Prereferral Intervention

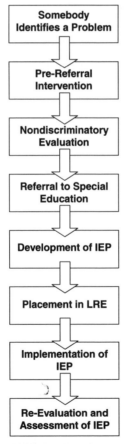

Figure 3.1. **The Special Education Process**

- Nondiscriminatory Evaluation
- Referral to Special Education
- Development of an Initial Individualized Education Program (IEP)
- Placement in the Student's Least Restrictive Environment (LRE)
- Implementation of the Student's Individualized Education Program
- Re-evaluation and Assessment of the Student's IEP

STEP 1: IDENTIFICATION OF A PROBLEM

No matter what disability or level of functioning a student has, entrance into the special education process begins when somebody feels that there is a problem. Sometimes this occurs when parents or teachers feel that there is something just "not right" with their child. Maybe the child is not walking by the correct age or her speech is slightly slurred or she has difficulties with mathematics or getting along with other children. Other times the problem is identified prior to the child's birth, such as when a doctor notices something wrong on prenatal tests.

Normally, the more serious the disability, the sooner it is diagnosed. Physical conditions, such as Down's Syndrome, also tend to be diagnosed very early in the child's life. Less obvious disabilities, such as Attention Deficit Hyperactivity Disorder (ADHD) or dyslexia, might be identified when the child becomes an adult. Or they may never be diagnosed at all.

STEP 2: PREREFERRAL INTERVENTION

Let's suppose that you have a child who you think has a disability. She has difficulty learning new tasks and is consistently behind her peers in most academic activities. Her teachers have noticed the problem too and have the same concerns that you have. So what happens now that the problem has been identified?

The next step is to attempt to determine what might be causing the problem. Before assuming that the problem is with your child (i.e., that she has a disability or is not trying), you must first rule out other factors, such as the teaching style of the educator or environmental distractions. To help in this step, special educators will often observe the student wherever the problem seems to be occurring. Based upon their observations, special educators will make suggestions that might help alleviate the problem. For example, they might suggest that the student be moved to the front of the room or that the regular educator should try to use more concrete examples when teaching.

STEP 3: NONDISCRIMINATORY EVALUATION

Now let's suppose that your child has been observed many times by different people. They have made several recommendations to the regular educator, but none have seemed to help your child learn better. What now?

The next step is to determine whether your child has a disability that adversely affects her education. As was discussed in Chapter 2, this is done through a multifaceted, nondiscriminatory process. Specifically, information on your child would need to be gathered in a systematic manner and involve:

- Multiple Sources
- Multiple Evaluators
- Multiple Environments
- An Extended Period Of Time

Multiple Sources

The evaluation process should involve multiple sources. For example, if teachers wanted to assess your child's intelligence, they should give more than just one IQ test. That way, if your child wasn't feeling well or was somehow distracted when taking the first test, the second test would show a discrepancy. As a result, there would be a better chance at catching erroneous scores.

Multiple sources are particularly important when behaviors are being assessed. For instance, suppose teachers thought that your child had Attention Deficit Hyperactivity Disorder (ADHD) and that they felt that she "frequently" got out of her chair (an important indicator that she may have ADHD). If your child was observed only once, teachers could not get a very clear idea as to the frequency of her actual behavior. Maybe she was particularly hyped up the day she was observed. Maybe she knew that she was being observed and that she was nervous, causing her to look more "antsy" than she normally would have been.

The underlying idea is that the more sources of information you have regarding your child, the truer the picture will be. However, it should be noted that you will never get a completely accurate picture of any child. All assessments have inherent biases. Further, how people interpret results often says more about them than the actual student being evaluated.

Multiple Evaluators

In addition to having multiple sources of information, your daughter's assessment should also involve multiple evaluators. This is so no one person is gathering all of the data. Having a second or third opinion could help provide broader insights as well as reduce the likelihood of bias. Multiple evaluators are particularly important when observations are required to make a diagnosis. After all, one person's rude child is another person's assertive child.

"Who should these evaluators be?" you might be asking. Certainly you want to have a diverse range of individuals. There should be people who know the child well and can lend valuable insight about him or her, such as the child's parent. There should also be individuals who are completely neutral and hold no preconceived notions about the child, such as a teacher who doesn't have the child as a student. Table 3.1 lists some of the people who could be used to help evaluate your child.

Multiple Environments

All assessments should be conducted with multiple evaluators and multiple sources of information. What else constitutes a non-discriminatory evaluation? The next important component involves multiple environments.

Let's suppose that your child is only having problems in one classroom. If this were the case, it would be unlikely she would have a

Table 3.1.   Possible Evaluators

Special Educators	Psychologists
Regular Educators	Outside Experts
Counselors	Parents
Social Workers	Siblings
Medical Personnel	Other Family Members
Classroom Aids/Paraprofessionals	Peers of the Student
Other School Personnel	The Student

Table 3.2.   Potential Environments for Evaluations

Regular Education Classrooms	During Lunch At School
Special Education Classrooms	In The Community
School Hallways	At Home
On The Playground	During Structured Activities
On The School Bus	During Unstructured Activities

disability. Disabilities usually don't just disappear and then reappear in only one environment. For this reason, it is very important to gather data in multiple environments. Does the child have problems on the school bus? During lunch? In the community? At home? These questions can only be answered if various people in these environments observe her. Table 3.2 lists possible environments in which a child could be evaluated.

Over an Extended Period of Time

Let's suppose that you and your child's teachers feel that a formal evaluation is in order to determine whether or not your child has a disability. Extensive information is gathered from multiple sources, by multiple evaluators, and in multiple environments. Does this mean that a non-discriminatory evaluation has been conducted? No.

Assessments must also be conducted over an extended period of time. If all of the information on your child was gathered on the same day, little could actually be learned. Maybe she simply had a bad day. Or the day was uncommonly good. For this reason, data should be gathered over several days, if not weeks.

STEP 4: REFERRAL TO SPECIAL EDUCATION

The following outcomes are likely to arise. The first is that the results are inconclusive. That is, it is unclear if she has a disability or not. Further, nobody can explain why she is having problems learning. If this is the case, more tests should be run until a better understanding of the student can be obtained.

The second possibility is the results indicate that she doesn't have a disability that warrants special education. For instance, maybe she has a slight vision impairment that is easily corrected by glasses or contacts. If this were the case, your child would not qualify for special education. As a result, she would not be referred to special education, and the process would stop here. This is a distinct possibility. After all, only approximately 30percent of students assessed for special education are actually found to have a disability that adversely affects their education (Turnbull, Turnbull, Shank, Smith, and Leal, 2002).

The final possibility is that the assessments indicate that she has a disability that adversely affects her ability to receive an appropriate public education. Perhaps she has mental retardation or a learning disability or a number of other conditions. In these situations, the child would be referred to special education, and a formal educational plan would be developed.

STEP 5: DEVELOPING EDUCATION PLANS

Educational plans are blueprints created by education teams, which consist of the student's parents, teachers, and any other people who might be involved with the student. In fact, the child should be part of the team if willing and able to participate.

Educational plans, such as Individualized Education Programs (or IEPs), outline what services are going to be provided to the student and by whom. They also specify the goals and objectives of these services as well as any special considerations that the student may need, such as accommodations for tests. In essence, they are a contract between the school and the parents about the education of the student. This "contract" is usually updated annually, but can be redeveloped as needed.

There are many different types of educational plans. Clearly the most common for students in special education is the Individualized Education Program (IEP). Every student in special education must have one according to federal law. However there are several other plans that students in special education might have in addition to their IEP, such as those presented in Table 3.3:

- Individualized Family Service Plan (IFSP)
- Individualized Health Care Plan (IHCP)
- Vocational Career Plan
- Differential Educational Plan
- 504 Plan
- Individualized Program Plan (IPP)
- Individualized Written Rehabilitation Plan (IWRP)

Table 3.3.   Summary of Educational Plans

Educational Plan	Summary
Individualized Education Program (IEP)	For all students in special education age 3 to 21.
Individualized Family Service Plan (IFSP)	For children younger that 3 and their families.
Individualized Health Care Plan (IHCP)	For students with significant health-related needs, such as catheters.
Vocational Career Plan	For students in high school vocational-preparation programs.
Differential Education Plan	For gifted or talented students in specialized enrichment programs.
504 Plan	For students who have disabilities that might not qualify for special education, such as wheelchair users.
Individualized Program Plan (IPP)	For adults with disabilities enrolled in programs, such as supported or sheltered employment.
Individualized Written Rehabilitation Plan (IWRP)	For individuals who are being served via vocational rehabilitation programs.

Individualized Education Programs (IEP)

Individualized Education Programs, or IEPs, are for all students enrolled in special education who are between the ages of three and twenty-one. IEPs are legally binding. That is, the services that the school promises to provide must be provided. How to develop IEPs will be discussed in Chapter 4.

Individualized Family Service Plans (IFSP)

When children are younger than three years old, they do not have IEPs. They have IFSPs, or Individualized Family Service Plans. Unlike IEPs, which only address the needs of the student, IFSPs attempt to focus on the family as a whole. For instance, IFSPs might outline resources that the parents could use, such as respite care or family training programs.

Individualized Health Care Plans (IHCP)

Often students in, and out of, special education have unique medical needs. Maybe they need to be tube fed or have colostomy bags. In such situations, the parents and school officials draw up documents that resemble IEPs. In fact, they may even be part of an IEP. They are called Individualized Health Care Plans (IHCPs) and outline the student's medical needs, what will be done during school hours, and by whom.

Vocational Career Plans

It is not uncommon for many students in special education to be enrolled in vocational training programs. Vocational programs could include what used to be called "shop classes" or they could be "work experiences" where students leave school for part of their school day and work in the community. Many regular education students participate in these programs.

Often vocational programs will have formalized plans of study, sometimes called Vocational Career Plans. These plans outline what courses and experiences students will need to take in order to graduate as well as be prepared to be employed. For instance, if a student was majoring in automobile repair, the plan might spell out that he take two courses on engines, one on bodywork, one on electrical systems, etc. These plans can be tailored to the student's interests. For example, the student might be interested in a specific aspect of automobile repair, such as fixing diesel truck engines. Unlike IEPs, these plans are not legally binding.

Differential Educational Plans

Remember, special education does not mean stupid. It is very important for people to realize that just because somebody is receiving special education services this does not mean that they aren't smart. In fact, many students with disabilities are also gifted or talented in some way. Just look at Albert Einstein or Stephen Hawkings. Albert Einstein had a learning disability and Stephen Hawkings is paralyzed as well as non-verbal, yet both of these people are (or were in Einstein's case) extremely intelligent.

Many students in special education who are cognitively gifted or talented will have formalized plans in addition to their IEP. These plans have many names, including Differential Educational Plans, Growth Plans, Acceleration Plans, and Achievement Plans. Basically, they are much like IEPs, but without the legal repercussions. They outline the goals of students and programmatic services the schools are willing to provide them. It is very possible that gifted students who are in special education will have some variation of these plans included with their IEP.

504 Plans

In addition to the Individuals with Disabilities Education Act (IDEA), Section 504 of the Rehabilitation Act is a key piece of legislation for people with disabilities. It protects people with disabilities from discrimination and provides them access to, among other things, education-related services.

Not everybody who qualifies for protection under 504 is entitled to special education. For example, a student with a missing limb may qualify as "disabled" under 504, but his disability does not adversely affect his ability to obtain an appropriate education, so he would not qualify for special education services. In these cases, students would have a 504 plan, which describes the services that the student would need at school, such as being given more time to get to and from classes.

Individualized Program Plans (IPP)

From ages birth to three, children have IFSPs. When they are three to age twenty-one, they have IEPs. So what happens when students become adults?

Some individuals with disabilities will enter adult service programs, such as sheltered workshops or supported employment programs. In these cases, they might have Individualized Program Plans, or IPPs. IPPs are very much like IEPs, but do not have legal obligations associated with them.

Individualized Written Rehabilitation Plans (IWRP)

Many people with disabilities qualify for services through vocational rehabilitation (VR). Just like special education programs, vocational rehabilitation programs have formalized plans that document the services that will be provided to program participants. These are called Individualized Written Rehabilitation Plans, or IWRPs. As with IPPs, IWRPs are not legally binding.

STEP 6: PLACEMENT IN THE STUDENT'S LEAST RESTRICTIVE ENVIRONMENT (LRE)

Imagine that your child has been diagnosed with a disability that adversely affects her ability to obtain an appropriate education. An IEP Team, of which you are a participating member, meets and creates an educational plan (or more than one). This plan outlines all of the goals and objectives that your daughter will be working on this year as well as all of the services that she will need to accomplish these goals. Now what?

The next step is to place your child in her least restrictive environment. As we discussed in Chapter 2, the least restrictive environment is different for each student. Not all students should be placed in the regular education classroom. Further, a student's LRE is not based upon IQ or disability label. Sometimes, students who are very smart are best placed in segregated classrooms, which can also happen to students with severe behavior problems. However, when identifying a student's LRE, the IEP team must first consider placing the student in the regular classroom and then justify their decision.

STEP 7: IMPLEMENTATION OF THE STUDENT'S IEP

Once your child is placed in her least restrictive environment, teachers now attempt to provide her a free and appropriate public education, or FAPE. They do this by carrying out activities designed to give your child the skills she needs to achieve her short-term objectives, and thus her annual goals—which will be discussed in Chapter 4.

Since each student has different needs and each student's IEP is based upon unique circumstances, how teachers teach special education students can vary widely from student to student. So, while your child's special education teacher might only have five students in his class, it is as if he is teaching five different classes of students.

STEP 8: REVIEW AND REEVALUATION OF THE IEP

A year has passed. Your child has achieved some of her goals and hasn't achieved others. What happens now?

According to IDEA, every student's IEP has to be reviewed at least once a year. During this time, the student should be reevaluated to see if she still qualifies for special education as well as what her new needs are. Based upon these new needs, a new IEP is developed by the IEP Team and the process of providing a free and appropriate public education continues.

But what if you wanted to develop a new IEP before the year is up? Are you allowed to? Yes. This is actually very common, especially when the needs of the student suddenly change. You would simply reconvene the IEP Team and explain why you think the current IEP should be modified. If the rest of the IEP Team does not agree at any point of this process, either you or the school could begin the due process procedures discussed in Chapter 2.

It should be noted that parents are not the only IEP Team members who can request that the IEP be rewritten early. Teachers can as well. For instance, they might begin to feel that your child is misdiagnosed or placed in the wrong classroom. In either case, they can call the IEP Team together and attempt to correct the problem.

APPLYING WHAT YOU HAVE LEARNED

Go back and review the case study at the beginning of the chapter. Reflect on what has been covered in the chapter and try to answer the questions after the case study. What did you learn?

Question #1: Was The Special Education Process Followed In J.R.'S Case Study?

Students don't suddenly become enrolled in special education. There is often a lengthy process that parents and educators must follow before students receive special education services. Did Dr. Johansen follow this process in J.R.'s case?

In the case study at the beginning of the chapter, Mrs. Reilly simply called the principal, expressed her concerns about her son, and J.R. was enrolled in special education. In real life this would not have been appropriate. Before J.R. was formally enrolled in special education, there would have been some prereferral interventions. Perhaps there is something that the regular education teacher could have done to minimize J.R.'s difficulties. Further, before he is enrolled in special education, a nondiscriminatory evaluation would need to be conducted, as we will discuss next.

Question #2: Did J.R. Receive A Nondiscriminatory Evaluation?

Before a student can be placed in special education, they must receive a nondiscriminatory evaluation. The results of this evaluation will be used to determine if a student is eligible for special education. That is, the evaluation will attempt to ascertain if the student has a disability that adversely affects their education. Did J.R. have a nondiscriminatory evaluation?

This is a hard question to answer. In order to have a nondiscriminatory evaluation, data on a student should be gathered using multiple instruments, in multiple environments, by multiple evaluations, over an extended period of time. J.R.'s pediatrician may have done all of this, but it is unlikely. She probably just asked Mrs. Reilly to fill-out a checklist to see if her son met the criteria for ADHD (which will be discussed in Chapter 5). If this was the case, then, no—J.R. did not have a nondiscriminatory evaluation.

Question #3: When Should J.R.'S IEP Be Re-Evaluated?

In the case study, the principal, Dr. Johansen, stated that J.R.'s IEP would be reevaluated "every few years." Is this correct? How often do IEPs have to be re-evaluated?

According to IDEA, IEPs must be reassessed at least annually. So Dr. Johansen is incorrect. Moreover, there is nothing stopping IEPs from being rewritten more frequently. This is often the case with students whose needs change before the year is up.

Question #4: Other Than An IEP, What Other Kinds Of Formal Plans Might J.R. Have?

According to IDEA, all students in special education must have an IEP or Individualized Education Program. However, there are many other plans that they can have. Other than an IEP, what other formal plans might students like J.R. have?

Since J.R. is in school, he could have an IHCP (if he had health concerns), a Vocational Career Plan (if he happened to be in a vocational program), a Differential Educational Plan (if he were in a gifted or talented program), a IWRP (if he was receiving services through vocational rehabilitation), or a 504 plan (if he qualified for services under Section 504 of the Rehabilitation Act). He would not have an IFSP, because he is too old. Nor would he have an IPP, because he is still in school and would probably not be involved in adult programs for people with disabilities, such as sheltered workshops.

CHAPTER 4

Developing Individualized Education Programs

CHAPTER OBJECTIVES

Upon completing this chapter, you should be able to:

1. Identify strategies for preparing for IEP meetings.
2. Identify strategies for making IEP meetings run smoother.
3. Identify strategies for after the IEP meeting is completed.
4. Identify the nine components of IEPs.
5. Develop annual goals for IEPs.
6. Develop short-term objectives for IEPs.

CASE STUDY: JULIE'S IEP MEETING

"Okay everybody, let's get started. I haven't had the pleasure to meet everybody yet. I am Mrs. Rosenfield, Julie's special educator. I will be coordinating her annual IEP meeting this year. I think a good way to begin is for all of us to go around the table, state who we are and indicate what areas Julie needs to work on this year. I'll start.

"I think Julie really needs to work on her acceptance of authority figures. She has a hard time complying with directions given to her by her teachers. And when she does, she often acts in an angry or defiant manner."

"Hi, everybody. I am Winnie Collins. I am Julie's regular educator. I agree. We need to work on Julie's behavior. But I am more concerned about her lack of academic progress. Maybe we could write a short-term objective like 'Julie will increase her reading and math abilities.' She is simply horrible at reading and math. We know she isn't retarded. She just isn't applying herself. Maybe we could send her to the resource room a couple hours every day where she can get the kind of intense support she apparently needs."

"I am Joyce. I am Julie's school counselor. I think that she should work on her poor social skills. She has very few friends and often acts inappropriately around other students. I think that we should make this her top priority."

"Well, I don't know about her social skills. I am the school's nurse. She is approaching the age where Julie will need to learn about feminine hygiene. Let's put something in her IEP about making her learn about how to take care of these issues."

"Certainly learning about feminine issues is important, but she will also have to continue working with me next year. Oh . . . hi. I am Steve, the school's speech and language therapist. Julie is still having a tremendously hard time articulating consonant blends. I think she should come to the speech and language room at least twice a week. She should come down more often, but I simply don't have the time."

"I'm Bert. Julie will have to keep going to the PT room as well. She still has considerable bilateral ancillary spasticity in her trunk and extremities due to her CP. If we don't improve her upper body strength, she will pretty much be a functional diplegiac, and she will need AT to get around. Her fine motor development is also substantially behind that of her peers. We might want to consider sending her to the OT. Maybe we could put that in her IEP or maybe develop an IHCP for her."

Everybody turned to Julie's parents, who were next around the table, but they simply stared into space with glazed over eyes.

CASE STUDY QUESTIONS

After reading the case study and the rest of this chapter, you should be able to answer the following questions:

1. How could have Julie's parents prepared for their daughter's IEP meeting?
2. Who apparently is missing from the IEP?
3. What is wrong with the short-term objective that Julie's regular education teacher proposed?
4. What could Julie's parents do after this meeting to help make the next meeting more effective?

INTRODUCTION

Perhaps the most important aspect of the special education process is the development of education plans, especially Individualized Education Programs (IEPs). You can imagine IEPs as the map through the special education maze. If they are written well, they can lead the student directly to where the student wants to go. If they are written poorly, they can waste the student's time and lead to bad ends. For this reason, this entire chapter is dedicated to creating effective IEPs. Specifically, the following topics will be discussed:

- Tips For Before The IEP Meeting
- Tips For During The IEP Meeting
- Tips For Developing The Actual IEP
- Tips For After The IEP Meeting

TIPS FOR BEFORE THE IEP MEETING

The beginning of the IEP process does not start when the IEP team meets. It starts long before. In order for the IEP team to do their job well, they must be prepared. Here are some suggestions that can help you prepare for you child's IEP meeting. Table 4.1 provides a checklist that you can use prior to your IEP meetings.

Review Past and Present IEPs

IEPs should build upon each other. The successes and shortcomings of the previous years should help guide what the present plan will say. So review the past and present IEPs. Ask yourself these questions:

- Are there unresolved issues that need to be carried over for next year? Why are they unresolved? Does your child need different supports or new teaching strategies in order to achieve these goals?
- Are unachieved previous goals still needed? Or have circumstances changed where the student no longer needs to focus on that skill?
- What goals has your child already mastered? Were the teaching strategies used for these goals effective?
- Do the goals from past IEPs build upon each other so that by the time the student exits school, she will be able to succeed in life?

Table 4.1.   Before the IEP Meeting Checklist

Preparing for your child's IEP meetings can be a bit overwhelming. Below is a simple checklist that you can use to prepare for these meetings. You may wish to add things relevant to your specific situation in the spaces provided at the bottom.

❑ Have you reviewed the present and past IEPs?
❑ Have you written down a list of goals and objectives that were not previously accomplished?
❑ Have you written down a list of goals and objectives that might be beneficial to work on for the next school year?
❑ Have you prioritized all of the goals and objectives that could be addressed?
❑ Have you written down a list of your child's strengths?
❑ Have you written down a list of areas in which your child could improve?
❑ Have you discussed the upcoming meeting with your child's teachers?
❑ Do you have a copy of the meeting's agenda?
❑ Have you considered who should attend the meeting?
❑ Have you invited everybody that you would like to attend the meeting, including the student?
❑ Is all of your information organized so it will be easy to find during the meeting?
❑ Has the meeting been scheduled at a mutually beneficial time and place?
❑ Do you need additional information prior to the meeting?
❑ _____
❑ _____
❑ _____

Write Down Potential Goals and Objectives for the Upcoming Year

Ideas come at the strangest times. Perhaps you will be falling asleep or driving on the freeway, regardless of where you are try to write down ideas for potential goals and objectives. Keep these ideas where you can find them when the time comes to renew your child's IEP. Perhaps keep a file with all the information and forms related to your child's IEP.

Prioritize Your Ideas for Goals and Objectives

Let's face it, we all have areas of our life we could improve. We could spend more time with friends and family. We could read more. We could clean the house more often. However, if we tried to work on everything that we could to, we probably wouldn't get much done. After all, time is limited.

The same is true for IEPs. There are so many different goals and objectives that your child could work on. He could be better at mathematics. He could make more friends. He could start planning for his future. He could participate more in class. The possibilities are endless. Unfortunately, the time and resources of teachers are not. So you will have to prioritize your ideas for future goals and objectives.

How do you prioritize? It sounds easy, but it isn't always. For example, how do you choose between learning functional math and acting more socially appropriate? Both are important in life, but your child may not have time to work on both at the same time. When trying to prioritize potential goals and objectives, start by asking yourself these questions:

- Are there goals that overlap? For example, maybe your child could work in small groups where he can make new friends and learn math at the same time.
- What are the underlying causes of multiple problems? For example, suppose that your child is frequently late for school, loses things, and doesn't complete his homework. Maybe the underlying cause for all these problems is that the student has a problem managing his time. So instead of three different goals (i.e., being on time, remembering where things are, and completing homework), perhaps one goal will take care of all these problems at once (e.g., learning to use a day planner.)
- Are there areas of immediate concern? Certainly if a student is suicidal, then mitigating depression and improving self-esteem are probably more important than preparing them for something that is many years off, such as entering college.
- Does your child have a preference as to what goals are included in the IEP? After all, it is the student's plan, not yours. Your child might have some keen insights that you haven't considered.

Discuss the Meeting with Other Team Members

If you are not running the meeting yourself, ask whoever is to send you a copy of the meeting's agenda well in advance. This will help you prepare for the topics that will be discussed. Further, it will give you an opportunity to discuss the upcoming meeting with other team members. Perhaps they can give you some of their insights or you could share yours. Pre-meeting discussions with other team members could help prevent unpleasant or time-consuming surprises.

Invite People Whom You Want to Attend the Meeting

Many people believe that special educators are in charge of conducting IEP meetings. While it is true that special educators traditionally run the proceedings, this does not mean that you can't invite whomever you want to attend. In fact, parents can invite anybody they wish. They can also prohibit people from attending IEP meetings. if they so desired.

It is often advantageous for parents to have friends or other family members attend meetings with them. Sometimes there is strength in numbers. Further, these other people might be able to help create an effective education plan. Official advocates who know about disabilities and the law can also be very beneficial when invited to IEP meetings. Advocates can be found through many of the organizations listed in Chapter 7.

Schedule the Meeting at an Appropriate Time and Location

Meetings don't have to be during the school day or at school. In fact, many parents work during the school day and can't afford to leave early. Further, schools are the "home turf" of the teachers. It can be intimidating for parents to have meetings at the school. If you wanted, you could have the meeting at a coffee shop or at your home on the weekend. Your child's teachers should attempt to accommodate your schedule and preferences. But please be considerate of everybody else's schedule. Not everybody wants to give up their weekends. Teachers have lives of their own too. Still, having a meeting over a cup of coffee or over dinner might make the time more enjoyable as well as productive.

Organize Your Thoughts and Materials

IEP meetings can be immensely nerve-wracking. So it is very likely that you will forget to say certain things that you wanted to say. To prevent this, have everything that you want to bring to the meeting organized. Have notes on every point that you want to make. Further, if you want to share information, such as a medical report from your child's doctor, have more than enough copies for everybody. Maybe even send the report to the other team members beforehand so that they can read it prior to the meeting. Being organized will help make the meeting run more efficiently and avoid wasted time.

Ask for More Information if Needed

Perhaps the key to helping students with disabilities is to understand their condition. If you do not know what oppositional defiant disorder (ODD), dyslexia, cerebral palsy (CP), or whatever your child's disability is, you should probably learn at least the basics. Chapter 5 discusses some of the more common disabilities that students in special education tend to have, including mental retardation, learning disabilities, behavior disorders, and attention deficit hyperactivity disorders. Chapter 7 lists many books, organizations, and websites where you can gain additional information. Also, do not be afraid to ask your child's teacher for resources. Teachers might be willing to lend you a special education textbook.

TIPS FOR DURING THE IEP MEETING

The big day finally arrives. You have researched your child's disability. You have reviewed various documents, such as past IEPs and medical reports, you have generated and prioritized a list of potential goal for your child. Now what?

Just imagine walking into a room with various special educators, regular educators, school psychologists, and school administrators. Each one presents reports about your child—focusing upon all the negative stuff. Moreover, they all tend to talk in some strange language (IEP, PLOP, LRE, MR, CP, LD, BD)! It is enough to make you want to go AWOL! Needless to say, these meetings can be very stressful for many parents (as well as for teachers and other team members). In this section of the chapter, we will discuss strategies to help you make the IEP meeting a rewarding and productive experience. Table 4.2 provides you with a checklist that could help you during your child's next IEP meeting.

Table 4.2.   During the IEP Meeting Checklist

IEP meetings can be very stressful, especially when there is a lot to cover. Here is a simple checklist that you can use to make sure that you don't forget anything. There are spaces at the bottom for you to add your own ideas.

❑ Offer to help in running the next meeting.
❑ Offer to help collect data on your child's progress.
❑ Schedule another meeting if more time is needed to think about all of the options.
❑ Ask people to explain information if needed.
❑ Share your thoughts regarding your child's strengths and areas of needs.
❑ Share your thoughts regarding possible goals and objectives.
❑ Work as a team.
❑ Take breaks as needed.
❑ Keep the purpose of the meeting in mind (helping your child succeed).
❑ Frequently restate perceptions to clarify meaning and to build consensus.
❑ _____
❑ _____
❑ _____

Offer to Help Run the Meeting

As mentioned earlier, there is nothing that says that the special education teacher has to run the meeting. If you want, you could volunteer to do it. This would enable you to participate more and to have greater control, but it will also reduce the amount of work that the special educator has to do—something that he or she might really enjoy! All of the same paperwork would still need to be filled out, but it would be up to you to organize everything and to type up the final plan.

Plan on Having Multiple Meetings

Don't expect to get everything done in one day. Having multiple meetings would also give you an opportunity to reflect on what is being said. Unfortunately, many professionals want to get the meeting over and done with. After all, they do have other students and families with whom they are working. However, having multiple meetings might actually save time. Think about it this way. One option is to have a long meeting where everybody debates their positions and tries to process all of the potential options available to them. An alternative is to have two short meetings where much of the processing is done in between the meetings.

Granted, sometimes it is best not to lose momentum. If the team is really working things out and getting a lot done, taking a break or stopping the meeting completely might be detrimental. Still, do not think that everything has to be done in one sitting. If you want time to consider everything that has been said, you are well within your rights to suggest meeting again at a later date. Who knows, maybe other team members want more time too!

Offer to Help Collect Data

Don't expect the teachers to do all of the work. Effective IEPs take a lot of planning and information gathering. Offer to collect data to see if the strategies being utilized are working. Maybe you could keep a journal of your child's behavior. Or perhaps you could graph your child's test scores. Anything that you do is something that somebody else doesn't have to do. Plus, it makes you a more active and needed part of the team.

Ask for Explanations

Clearly, developing IEPs is a daunting task. But you can't be afraid to ask for people to explain things. Educators simply forget that not everybody knows what various terms mean. Remember, you are planning your child's future. Get involved and ask questions if you need explanations.

Share Your Thoughts

Don't wait for somebody to ask what you think. Share your perspective, concerns, and opinions. It might be scary for you to speak up in a room full of professionals, but you do have a valid point of view. After all, who knows your child better than you do? Just because you do not have a degree in special education, doesn't mean that your observations and ideas are not pertinent.

Be a Team Member

Being a member of a team means more than speaking your mind. In fact, it might also mean that you have to bite your tongue from time to time. If the IEP meeting gets tense, try to remember that most educators care a great deal about their profession and their students. If there is a difference of opinion, it is probably just because people have different points of view—not because they don't like you or your child. When being a team member, try to follow these simple rules (other strategies for effective collaboration and team building are presented in Chapter 6):

- Agree to disagree on unimportant matters.
- Listen to what people have to say before you begin formulating your reply.
- Ask others to clarify their positions if you are unclear about what they actually mean.
- Try to look at the issues from other people's perspectives.
- Never think of an idea as being bad. Think of ways to make it better.
- Keep the purpose of the meeting in mind. You are all there to help a child succeed. Write that down and put it on the wall if need be. Sometimes we forget what all of this is all about.

- Offer to help out as much as possible—collect data, offer to organize the next meeting, bring refreshments, etc.

TIPS FOR DEVELOPING THE ACTUAL IEP

Please keep in mind that IEPs (and other educational plans discussed in Chapter 3) should be written by the team as a whole, not just by the special educator or school administrator (see Figure 4.1 for a sample IEP form). Teachers and other team members might have notes or reports typed up at the time of the meeting, but the final document approved by the team should be a combined effort of everybody involved. Parents, and other team members, have a right to have their input included within the IEP.

Individualized Education Program (IEP)

Student: ___ James Rich _____   DOB: _9/14/90___   Grade : _ 8th_

Present Level of Performance (PLOP) [how the disability affects the student's ability to progress through the general education curriculum]	Special Education, Related Services, Accommodations, and Modifications [frequency, duration, and location]	Annual Goals and Short-Term Objectives [Condition, Target Behavior, and Criterion]
Several standardized tests indicate that James is 2.4 grade levels behind his peers in mathematics. Specifically, while he is able to perform two-digit addition and subtraction problems, he has difficulty correctly answering two-digit multiplication and division problems.	James will receive tutoring for math each day for 30 minutes in the learning resource room. James will take his math tests in the learning resource room. James will be given an extra 45 minutes on all math exams. James can use a calculator on all math assignments.	Annual Goal #1 James will improve his math abilities Short-Term Objective #1.1 When given a math assignment with double-digit multiplication and division problems, James will correctly answer 50% of the math problems by November 1st. Short-Term Objective #1.2 When given a math assignment with double-digit multiplication and division problems, James will correctly answer 75% of the math problems by January 1st.

		Short-Term Objective #1.3 When given a math assignment with double-digit multiplication and division problems, James will correctly answer 90% of the math problems by May 1st.

Least Restrictive Environment: James will be placed in the general education classroom the entire day with the exception of during math period where he will be taught in the learning resource room. The IEP Team feels that full inclusion within the general education classroom would not provide James with the support in math that he requires.

Transition-Related Services: The IEP Team does not wish to address transition-related services at this time.

Participation in State and District-Wide Tests: James will participate fully in all state and district-wide assessments, however, he will be given an extra 45 minutes on all tests involving mathematics.

Parental Notification: Mr. and Mrs. Rich will be contacted by phone during each full week of school. They will be appraised of James' progress and asked for their input during this time.

Signatures and Dates:		
_____	_____	_____
Parents	*School Representative*	*Student*
_____	_____	_____
Other Team Members	*Other Team Members*	*Other Team Members*

***Figure 4.1.* Sample IEP Form**

Note: This is just an example of how an IEP could look like. There are many different forms that schools use. Further, IEPs can be very lengthy, even as many as twenty or thirty pages, and have many goals and objectives. The sample provided is only meant to give you a visual image of how all the components discussed in the chapter can come together.

IEPs can be very complex and intimidating to parents as well as teachers. They comprise nine components. Each of these is discussed in the sections below and in Table 4.3.

- Present Level of Performance (PLOP)
- Annual Goals
- Short-Term Objectives
- Special Education and Related Services
- Projected Dates, Duration, Frequency, and Location of Services

Table 4.3. Summary of IEP Components

IEP Component	Summary
Present Level of Performance (PLOP)	This provides an overview of the student's current abilities, including strengths and areas of weaknesses.
Annual Goals	These are broad statements of what the IEP team hopes that the student will achieve by the end of the school year.
Short-Term Objectives	These are the activities that the student will need to complete in order to accomplish each annual goal.
Special Education and Related Services	This lists the services that the student will receive during the school year.
Projected Dates, Duration, Frequency, and Location of Services	This indicates when, where, and for how long services will be provided to the student.
Least Restrictive Environment (LRE)	This states precisely where the student will be taught (e.g., the regular education classrooms, special education resource room, etc.)
Modification for State and District-Wide Assessments	This lists the supports, if any, that the student will need to participate in state and district-wide assessments.
Parental Notification	This explains in what manner and how frequently parents will be notified regarding their child's progress.
Transition Planning	This addresses the student's preparation for their movement to post-school outcomes, such as becoming employed or living independently in the community.

- Least Restrictive Environment (LRE)
- Modification for State and District-Wide Assessments
- Parental Notification
- Transition Planning

Present Level of Performance (PLOP)

Usually the first component that appears on IEPs is the Present Level of Performance, or PLOP. The PLOP sets the stage for the rest of the plan. It summarizes what various assessments have learned about the student, including the student's strengths and weaknesses. It also explains how the student's disability is affecting his or her ability to succeed in regular education.

Note that not all of your daughter's abilities are discussed in the PLOP. For instance, the PLOP does not have to mention that she can or can't tie her shoes. Only information relevant to the student's current educational plan is usually included.

Also note that information is presented as objectively and positively as possible. This is not always easy to do, but it can be done. For instance, suppose that your daughter is frequently out of her seat talking to her peers. Somebody could write a PLOP that says, "Becky never sits in her chair and is constantly bothering her peers." However, this is very negative and also not true. "Never" and "constantly" are absolute terms that do not apply in most situations. Plus, the term "bothering" is very negative. A more positive way of writing this section of the PLOP could be "Becky is a very social girl who likes to talk to her classmates. Teaching her when it is appropriate to socialize with her friends would enhance her social skills."

The idea is not to sugarcoat the facts or misrepresent the truth, but to create a positive view of the student. After all, this is somebody's child. How would you like to sit through a several hour-long IEP meeting hearing nothing but negative comments about your daughter? "She can't do this! She can't do that!" An extensive flow of negative statements can create a barrier between teachers and parents. This barrier will only hurt the student and her ability to get an appropriate education. Thinking positive promotes positive behavior.

Annual Goals

Annual goals and short-term objectives create the body of the educational plan. These will guide how a free and appropriate public education will be achieved. They also guide what and how teachers will teach.

Annual goals are brief, broad statements of what the IEP team wants the student to accomplish by the time the IEP is re-evaluated. They must be based upon the needs and interests of the individual student. Further, they must be positive. For example, the annual goal "Richard will stop asking stupid questions" is not positive.

Examples of appropriate annual goals include:

- "Billie will increase his reading ability."
- "Susie will improve her social skills."
- "James will improve his math skills."

Short-Term Objectives (STO)

Short-term objectives or STOs are the steps that the student will take to achieve each annual goal. Each annual goal will have several short-term objectives, which are also called benchmarks. For example, the annual goal "Billie will increase his reading ability" might have the following short-term objectives:

- "When presented with flash cards, Billie will read the word on the flash card aloud with 90 percent accuracy by November 1st."
- "When presented with flash cards, Billie will read the word on the flash card aloud with 100 percent accuracy by December 1st."
- "When given a passage at his reading level, Billie will read the past aloud with 100% by December 15th."
- "When given a worksheet measuring the comprehension of a passage just read, Billie will correctly answer in writing 9 out of 10 questions."

Good short-term objectives have three important components:

- Condition
- Target Behavior
- Criterion

• *Condition.*   Short-term objectives have three components. The first is the condition. This is when the behavior is going to occur. For example, "when given an assignment . . .", "when instructed by the teacher . . .", and "upon receiving a compliment . . ." are all conditional phrases. Conditions give teachers a guideline for when to assess whether objectives have been achieved. Without conditions, it is unclear when the student is supposed actually to perform the target behavior.

Target behavior.   The second component of short-term objectives is the actual target behavior the student is expected to perform. There are three elements of appropriately written target behaviors:

- The behavior is performed by the student, not the teacher.
- Only one behavior is included per objective.
- The behavior is measurable.

Consider the short-term objective "When Glen gets out of his seat, he will be sent to time out by the teacher." This is not a good objective because the target behavior (i.e., being sent to time out) is actually being done by the teacher, not by Glen.

How about the short-term objective, ". . . Nancy will read a passage and underline each vocabulary word . . ."? What is wrong with it? It has two behaviors—reading and underlining. What would happen if Nancy could underline very well, but could not read? She would not achieve her objective and, as a result, people might assume that she could neither read nor underline, thus giving an inaccurate impression.

Finally, the target behavior has to be measurable so that there is no question as to whether or not the student accomplished the objective. Suppose that a short-term objective included the phrase ". . . John will pay attention. . . ." How would you measure paying attention? John could be looking right at the teacher, nodding his head, but that does not mean he is paying attention. Consequently, in order to be measurable, the behavior must be observable.

Let's suppose that a short-term objective stated that a student will ". . . try to act appropriately." What is wrong with this objective? First, acting appropriately is not measurable. Different people could watch a student and have a different definition of the term "appropriately." So, if teachers do not have a clear idea of what is expected, the student is probably going to be confused as well. In other words, an ambiguous objective can set the student up for failure.

Secondly, the objective says that the student will "try" to act appropriately. Trying is not observable. Suppose that the student hit another child with a baseball bat and he said, "Well I tried to act appropriately." Could you prove that he didn't try? Moreover, goals and objectives are only concerned with what a student does, not what they try to do or what they want to do.

Criterion.   The final component of a short-term objective is the criterion. The criterion is the ruler by which a student's actions are measured to see whether the objective has been achieved. Examples of criteria include ". . . 100 percent of the time . . ." and ". . . 9 out of 10 math problems. . . ."

Objectives can also be written so that the criterion is implied. For example, an objective could read "When instructed by her teacher (the condition), Kristen will write a report about a job she will like to have when she is an adult (the target behavior)." Kristen either writes the report or she doesn't. You can't write a report with 75% accuracy.

You might be asking, "How high should a criterion be?" The answer is "it depends." Some students might get discouraged if they don't succeed right away. For these students, setting a series of easy-to-achieve objectives might be best. Other students might not try if they think that their objectives are beneath their abilities. For these students, you might want to set more challenging criteria.

Special Education and Related Services

Another section of your child's IEP must clearly state what services that she will receive in order to attain her annual goals. There are two types of services that students can access—special education services and related services. Each is described below.

Special education services.   Special education services are the services that come as a result of being in special education. They might include an aide who helps the student with her homework. Or it could involve specific teaching strategies that the regular educator uses to teach the student new skills.

Related services.   Related services are services that certain students may need in order to benefit from special education. For example, some students might need physical therapy or counseling. They might also need transportation to and from school. Not every student in special education will need related services, but those who do are guaranteed them under IDEA at no additional cost to the parents.

Projected Dates, Frequency, Location, and Duration of Services

In addition to the services that your child will be receiving, IEPs must also list:

- the projected start dates of services (e.g., September 1st)
- how frequently services will be provided (e.g., two times per week)
- location where services will be provided (e.g., in the resource room or guidance counselor's office)
- duration of these services (e.g., an hour)

Least Restrictive Environment (LRE)

IEPs also need to indicate where the student will be taught, such as in a self-contained classroom or in the regular education classroom. As we discussed in Chapter 2, IDEA guarantees that students be taught in the least restrictive environment (LRE) possible. Not only does the IEP have to explain exactly where the student will be taught, but it also has to explain why the student is not taught in the regular classroom all of the time. For example, there might be a simple statement that says, "The IEP team concluded that full-time placement within the regular education classroom would not match Susie's educational needs. She will be taught within a resource room for all subjects with the exception of art and music, in which she will participate with her non-disabled peers."

Modifications for State or District-Wide Assessments

IEPs must also outline the modifications to state and district-wide assessments the student will need. It may be that the IEP Team feels that taking these assessments are not beneficial for the student, such as students with profound mental retardation. In such cases, the IEP team would simply include a justification for their decision to exclude the student from testing. Or maybe the student will need extra time or an aide who will read the test aloud. In either case, these modifications must be written into the IEP.

Parental Notification

According to IDEA, parents have the right to be informed of their child's progress. So the IEP must contain a statement of how and how frequently parents will be contacted. There is no set frequency or method. The law states only that parents of special education students need to be informed at least as much as parents of students without disabilities. A sentence saying something like "The parents will be contacted in writing at the end of each school week" would be sufficient.

Transition Planning

One of the latest trends to influence special education is transition planning. Transition is often thought of as the movement from school to work, or school-to-adult life. However, it probably is better to think of it as preparing students for changes that will occur throughout their life.

According to IDEA, transition must be addressed in every student's IEP by age fourteen and each year thereafter. At this time, IEPs must have goals that involve the movement from school to adult outcomes, including:

- Postsecondary education
- Vocational training
- Employment
- Independent living
- Community participation

You might be asking, "What if I want my child to start working on transition-related skills before she turns fourteen? Is that possible?" Yes. Remember, that the law says that transition must be addressed by age fourteen. So if you want to have your child taught transition skills before then, you certainly can. In fact, many authors recommend that all goals should in some way prepare students for their future. This is particularly appropriate for students who may need extra time to learn skills, such as students with severe or multiple disabilities.

Another question is "What if I want to have goals written for areas not listed above?" For example, maybe you want your daughter to be taught about sex or menstruation. Can you include these in an education plan? Yes. You can have these written into the IEP whenever you want, just like any other goal. You do not have to wait for a certain age.

There is one more consideration regarding transition and IEPs. By the time your daughter reaches the age of majority, she must be notified of her rights as an adult. In most states, the age of majority is 18, but you might want to see what it is where you live.

TIPS FOR AFTER THE IEP MEETING

So you, your child's teachers, and maybe even your child, are all finally done with the IEP. It took a lot of give and take, but in the end all of your hard work paid off. You now have a clear plan that will help your child prepare for the future. Is the IEP process finished? Nope! Not by a long shot. In fact, the hard part has just begun!

Table 4.4.   Checklist for after the IEP Meeting

Remember, that the IEP process is not over after everybody leaves the meeting. Now the hard work begins! Here is a checklist outlining some of the activities that you might need to perform after the meeting. There are spaces at the bottom for you to add your own ideas.

❏ Maintain regular communication regarding the student's progress as well as teacher/parental concerns.
❏ Thank team members for their participation.
❏ Regularly thank team members for their efforts.
❏ Attend conferences and meetings of professional organizations.
❏ Network with other parents.
❏ Collect data on student progress.
❏ _____
❏ _____
❏ _____

Actually carrying out the IEP is far more important (and often more difficult) than writing it. Further, just as it is up to the team as a whole to write the IEP, it is up to the team to implement it. Don't leave all the dirty work for the teachers. Remember, everybody is on the same team. Share the work and the rewards! Here are some suggestions (see Table 4.4 for a post-IEP meeting checklist).

Thank Team Members for Their Help

Like being a parent, teaching is often a thankless job. Children do not usually say to their teachers and parents, "Thank you for making me do my homework so I can succeed later on in life." Instead, they usually complain and grumble. So take a few minutes every few weeks and thank the people who are helping you help your child. Send a card or make a quick phone call. Maybe even give them small gifts like flowers every now and again. If they know that you appreciate their work, they will probably work with you even better than they do now. Plus, it is just plain nice.

Keep Regular Contact with Other Team Members

All too often, parents and teachers communicate only during IEP meetings and during parent-teacher conferences. This is not enough contact to maintain positive teams. How can teachers get to know their students if they do not know their students' families? So contact members of the IEP team regularly. Send notes back and forth from school. Use e-mail. Perhaps even keep a running journal that you can send them every week. Keep the lines of communication open any way you can.

Ongoing communication is important because the needs of children can change quickly and frequently, especially when children have disabilities. Consequently, you may have to update your child's IEP before the year is up. Imagine how you would feel if your child's teacher suddenly called you out of the blue and said, "Your child is doing horribly! We need to change everything! When can you meet?" This would be a shock if you thought your child was doing well.

Moreover, teachers need to know if there are changes in the child's life. For example, they will need to know if your child is on a new type of medication, so they can watch for side effects. Simply put, a team cannot be very effective if its members do not communicate regularly.

Join Professional Organizations

Special education, like children, changes quickly. Laws are constantly being revised or interpreted in new ways. New disabilities are being "discovered," and old ones are being redefined. Further, promising medical advances and treatments are published almost daily. For these reasons, it is important for parents (and teachers) to keep up on the latest developments.

One way to stay informed is to join professional organizations. Most organizations have newsletters and websites where you can update your knowledge. They also may put on an annual conference or have local chapters near your home. A list of several national organizations can be found in Chapter 7.

Help Support Other Families

It isn't enough for parents to educate themselves about their child's disability and to participate in their own IEPs. Parents have a responsibility of sharing their knowledge and experiences with other families, especially those who do not have much hope or understanding of what is happening to them. One way that parents can help each other is to join support groups. Here they can network and share stories and resources, such as which doctors in the area are the best or where to get information. Boxed Discussion 4.1 presents ways of forming support groups for parents and students with disabilities.

Collect Data

The education of students does not occur only at school, it occurs at home and in the community as well. Parents need to keep track of their child's accomplishments, if only to see the progress that they are making. Further, focusing on the positives can help alleviate some of the stress that accompanies having a child with special needs.

By collecting data on their child's performance, parents can also help inform teachers as to the success of their efforts. Clearly, if the child's behavior is getting worse, or she is not learning what she is being taught, the child's teachers might want to try different

---

Boxed Discussion 4.1:   Forming A Support Group

No matter how good of a person, or how knowledgeable, you are, there will be times when people learn more from their peers than they can ever learn from you. Let's face it. What you know about your child's disability is most likely comes from books, your college courses, or through observing your children. Unless you actually have the disability, your knowledge is rather limited. It is like you are trying to explain to a mother what it is like to give birth when you never have had a baby yourself. You can quote statistics and share your observations, but in many ways you have no idea what you are talking about. It is for this reason why support groups are so important and effective.

There are several national organizations and support groups for individuals with disabilities and their families (see Chapter Seven). There are probably local and state chapters of these groups within you community. However, you may wish to help your child or your family members form a support group of their own. Here are several ways you can get started:

- Host regularly occurring get-togethers or workshops for the family members or children who have disabilities. Allow time for participants to socialize and get to know each other.
- Start a newsletter and solicit help from other parents or family members. Perhaps they could share tips and resources with the other readers.
- Build linkages to other schools and grade levels. For instance, if your child is in middle school, invite parents of student who are currently in elementary or high school to your functions.
- Join national organizations and see if they will help you form a local chapter of their group.
- Start a web page or chat room where other people can learn more about your group.

Source: Cimera, R.E. (2002). *Teaching Superman How To Fly: Making ADHD A Gift.* Lanham, MD: Scarecrow Education Press.

Boxed Discussion 4.2:   The Responsibilities of Parents of Students in Special Education

In addition to be given many legal rights, there are many responsibilities that parents of students in special education have. These responsibilities should not be taken lightly. Remember, the education of your child is not just in the hands of teachers.

- Parents should participate actively in the education of their child.
- Parents should ask questions.
- Parents should treat other IEP team members with respect (remember the golden rule!)
- Parents should research their child's condition.
- Parents should become active members of the disabled community and share their knowledge with others.
- Parents should keep copies of all relevant records and data.
- Parents should not sign an IEP unless they understand and agree with it.
- Parents should attempt to solve problems before they start (be proactive!)
- Parents should develop cooperative relationships with their child's teachers and other IEP team members (collaboration is a two-way street!)

---

strategies. But teachers and parents can't know what is going on without data.

Monitoring children in-between IEPs is particularly important if a child is on medication. Most medications have adverse side effects. Some of these are very serious, such as brain, kidney, and liver damage. By collecting data on a regular basis, parents can help doctors see if the medication is working or hurting the child.

APPLYING WHAT YOU HAVE LEARNED

Go back and review the case study at the beginning of the chapter. Reflect on what has been covered in the chapter and try to answer the questions after the case study. What did you learn?

Question #1: How Could Have Julie's Parents Prepared For Their Daughter's IEP Meeting?

Having a successful IEP meeting involves preparation. It is difficult to just show up to such an important event and expect things to go well. So what could Julie's parents prepared for their meeting?

Perhaps one thing that Julie's parents could have done is found out beforehand who was going to be at the meeting. Then they could have contacted them prior to the meeting and saved time with the introductions. They could have also been sent each person's report so that they would have time to reflect upon all of the information being presented.

Question #2: Who Apparently Is Missing From The IEP?

Of course there are probably an infinite number of people who could be at IEP meetings. For example, Julie's pastor or medical doctor could have been there. But who, in particular, should be there?

There is no mention of Julie being at the meeting. Now certainly, not every student should be at their IEP meeting. For example, students who are too young to understand what is happening might not benefit from attending. However, Julie is apparently entering adolescence. She should be there if only to keep the purpose of the meeting in people's mind. After all, the IEP team is there to help her. She should have some input into what is being done.

Question #3: What Is Wrong With The Short-Term Objective That Julie's Regular Education Teacher Proposed?

Go back and look at the short-term objective that Julie's regular educator proposed. It stated that "Julie will increase her reading and math abilities." What is wrong with this objective?

First of all, it is more of an annual goal than a short-term objective. If you remember, annual goals are broad outcomes that you want your student to achieve at the end of the year. Short-term objectives are comprised within each annual goal. Increasing Julie's reading and math abilities is more of a long-term outcome, not something that can be done in a brief period of time.

Secondly, the objective contains two separate behaviors. Good objectives, and goals, should only have one observable behavior. In this particular case, Julie should have two annual goals, one focusing on math, the second on her reading abilities.

Finally, good objectives contain three components—the target behavior, criterion, and condition. As mentioned, there are too many target behaviors for this to be a good objective. Further, there is no condition (e.g., When given a worksheet on math . . .) or criterion (Julie will answer 80 percent of her math problems correctly).

Question #4: What Could Julie's Parents Do After This Meeting To Help Make The Next Meeting More Effective?

Remember, the IEP process doesn't end with the formation of the IEP document. So, what should Julie's parents do once the meeting was over? Here are a few suggestions.

- Thank everybody for his or her help. This could help Julie's parents get to know all of the many people who are involved in their daughter's education.
- Research their child's disability and current issues related to her education.
- Collect information to determine if the IEP is suiting Julie's needs.
- Remain in contact with team members.

CHAPTER 5

Very Basic Information Regarding Common Disabilities

CHAPTER OBJECTIVES:

By the end of this chapter, you should be able to:

1. Describe the diagnostic criteria for mental retardation, learning disabilities, behavior disorders, attention deficit hyperactivity disorder
2. Explain the differences between mental retardation and learning disabilities
3. Describe various conditions associated with mental retardation
4. List types of learning disabilities, behavior disorders, and attention deficit hyperactivity disorders

CASE STUDY: DIAGNOSING MARY MAGER

"I think," began Dr. Hernandez with a slight sigh. "After collecting a great deal of information from different sources, in different environments, from different people, and over an extended period of time, I think that we finally have enough data to determine what is going on with your daughter."

Mr. and Mrs. Mager shifted forward eagerly in their seats. Their daughter, Mary, stared off into space, twirling her hair, appearing not to care about the conversation.

"Well," Mr. and Mrs. Mager pressed. "What is it? What is wrong with her?" They said together.

Dr. Hernandez handed them each a copy of his report. It was quite thick and contained many tables and graphs. The Magers looked at it somewhat in awe and in fear.

"We tested Mary's IQ three times using three separate assessment devices. In each case, her IQ was slightly above normal." To this Mary raised one eyebrow. "Her IQ scores averaged about 118. Most people have IQs between 85 and 115, with the average being 100." Dr. Hernandez pointed to a graph of a bell-like object and then continued.

"I also gave Mary several standardized tests examining her abilities in various subjects. As you can see, she scored above grade level in reading and spelling, but well below her peers in mathematics. In fact, she is about three and a half grade levels behind."

Mary rolled her eyes and shifted uncomfortably in her seat.

"That is pretty consistent with the grades that she has been getting in her math classes over the past few years." Mr. Mager observed.

"Yes." Dr. Hernandez nodded. "Further, I observed Mary in several of her classes and in the hallway. I also asked each of her teachers to complete checklists regarding her behavior. We all agree that she usually is very polite and good-natured, although she does seem to get upset about poor performance in her math courses. She seems to pay attention and genuinely tries in her classes. . . ."

"See!" Mary explained sharply looking at her parents.

"Then why is she having so much difficulty passing math? She does so well in her other classes. What is wrong?"

CASE STUDY QUESTIONS

After reading the case study and the rest of this chapter, you should be able to answer the following questions:

1. Does Mary have mental retardation?
2. Does Mary have a behavior disorder?
3. Does Mary have an attention deficit hyperactivity disorder?
4. Does Mary have a learning disability?

INTRODUCTION

Thus far we have talked about what special education is, how it is different from regular education, laws that govern special education, and the special education process. In this chapter, we will discuss some of the common disabilities that students in special education have. Specifically, we will cover the definitions, defining characteristics, and potential ways of assessing:

- Mental Retardation
- Learning Disabilities
- Behavior Disorders
- Attention Deficit Hyperactivity Disorders (ADHD)

MENTAL RETARDATION

As it does with most of the disabilities we will be discussing, the public tends to misunderstand what mental retardation is and how it affects people. For instance, you may often hear on the news that somebody with mental retardation functions like a "three-year-old" or some age well below their actual age. This is extremely misleading. People with mental retardation aren't eternal children. They have the same biological urges that adults with "normal" IQs have. They are adults who have difficulty learning. Perhaps it would be helpful if we defined mental retardation and went on from there.

Defining Mental Retardation

Defining mental retardation is problematic for many reasons. First, there are many definitions proposed by various psychological and governmental organizations. Second, mental retardation is fundamentally associated with the concept of intelligence, which has changed drastically over the past few years. Still, there are three components to most definitions of mental retardation.

- Sub-average intelligence
- Poor adaptive skills
- Age of onset

Sub-average intelligence.   The most obvious and universal component used to define mental retardation is a sub-average intelligence. Simply put, people with mental retardation have lower intelligence than the rest of the population. This is not to say that they can't learn. They can. They merely process and recall information less efficiently than most of us. As a result they may need more time or more concrete instruction than do others. In order for you to understand mental retardation, you must first understand the concept of intelligence.

There are many, many different theories of intelligence and how humans learn. Suffice to say that no one theory pleases everybody. In fact, some people believe that intelligence cannot be measured at all or that IQ tests only examine book knowledge, which is different from intelligence. This, of course, is a gross simplification of a very complicated topic; however, it might help you think of intelligence as a measure of how efficiently we learn—not what we can learn. There are some people who can look at a math problem and get the answer right away. It is intuitive to them. There are other people who need extra help or more examples before they can see the answer. But everybody can learn, given enough time and effective teaching, even people with profound mental retardation.

Now look at the bell-shaped curve presented in Figure 5.1. This is a traditional representation of what some people believe the distribution of intelligence within the general population looks like. That is, there is a relatively small percentage of people who have really high IQs and can learn very quickly (to the far right of the curve). There is also a relatively small percentage of people who have great difficulty learning (to the far left of the curve). The majority fall somewhere in the middle, where the curve is at its tallest.

People with mental retardation score at the very bottom of this curve. Specifically, if 100 is the average IQ (represented by the line dissecting the bell-shaped curve in the middle), people with mental retardation have IQs below 70 to 75, depending upon the IQ test and definition of mental retardation utilized. In other words, approximately 2 percent of the population falls below the line that denotes mental retardation.

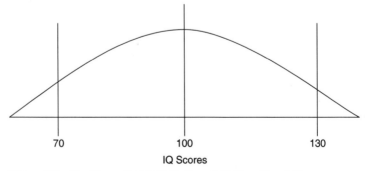

70   100   130
IQ Scores

Figure 5.1. **The Theoretical Distribution of IQs in a Population**

So why is the cut-off for mental retardation in the 70s? Why not at 90 or 50? To be completely honest, the cut-off is completely arbitrary. In fact, over the years, it has move considerably. Years ago, a student with an IQ of 80 would be considered mentally retarded. The same student today, however, would be considered "low average."

The point is that "sub-average intelligence" and "mental retardation" represent concepts based on arbitrary criteria, which are changeable. What is considered mental retardation today probably won't be mental retardation tomorrow. Here is an example.

Suppose that scientists identify the genes that control intelligence. As a result, through genetic engineering, everybody's IQ doubles. So if you have an IQ of 100 (which is average), your IQ would now be 200. What percent of the population would have mental retardation after the scientists have made everybody twice as "smart"?

The answer is "roughly 2%", the same as it is now. You see, mental retardation is not only an arbitrary concept, but it is also relative to the intelligence of everybody else in the population. If you double everybody's IQ, the cut-off for what is considered mental retardation would simply double too. So, in a future where intelligence might be genetically engineered, people with an IQ of 140 could be considered mentally retarded, even though those people would be considered "gifted" today.

Poor adaptive skills.   One of the main components of defining mental retardation is sub-average intelligence. Unfortunately, this is all relative to what people consider to be "sub-average." But intelligence is not the only defining factor of mental retardation. To have mental retardation, you must also have poor adaptive skills. More precisely, people need to have significant limitations in two or more of the following areas:

- Communication
- Self-Care
- Home Living
- Social Skills
- Community Use
- Self-Direction
- Health and Safety
- Functional Academics
- Leisure
- Employment

What exactly constitutes a "significant limitation"? That is a great question. Unfortunately, there is no clear answer. 'Appropriate' social skills are often determined by culture or situation. People of some cultures might stand closer to people than do people from other cultures. Or they may talk louder, interrupt more, or make gestures that other people believe are rude. Still, people with mental retardation tend to have noticeably impaired skills in multiple areas.

Age of onset.   So, in order to have mental retardation, somebody has to have a sub-average IQ (usually below 70 or 75) and poor adaptive skills in two or more of the areas listed above. There is one more important component when defining mental retardation—age of onset.

Mental retardation is thought to be inherent within the person. It isn't something that somebody develops over time. So, according to the most used definitions of mental retardation, mental retardation must manifest itself before age 18. That is, the person must have poor adaptive skills and sub-average intelligence before then. So, theoretically, if an average 30 year-old adult gets into a car accident, hits her head and suffers a traumatic brain injury that lowers her IQ to 50, she would not qualify as mentally retarded.

Characteristics of Students with Mental Retardation

It is difficult to describe students with mental retardation because it is such a multifaceted condition. Students with mild mental retardation are likely to have different abilities and issues than those with profound or severe mental retardation (see Table 5.1 for classifying the severity of mental retardation). Further, students with mental retardation are likely to have several coexisting disabilities at the same time, such as autism or Down's Syndrome, some of which will be discussed below.

Table 5.1.   Classification of Mental Retardation Severity

Classification	IQ Range
Borderline Mental Retardation	70 to 75
Mild Mental Retardation	50–55 to 70
Moderate Mental Retardation	35–40 to 50–55
Severe Mental Retardation	20–25 to 35–40
Profound Mental Retardation	Below 20–25

Note: There are many different ways of classifying the severity of mental retardation. The one presented is probably one of the most common. To learn about others, please consult the resources presented in Chapter 7.

Despite its diverse nature, there are many characteristics that students with mental retardation might display. Each is discussed below. Please keep in mind that not every student with mental retardation will have all of these characteristics. Like every other person, individuals with mental retardation have unique needs and attributes.

Abstract reasoning. One of the common characteristics of students with mental retardation is that they tend to have difficulty with abstract reasoning. They usually are very concrete learners. That is, they have to see what they are learning. For instance, math is very abstract. Telling a child with mental retardation that "2 + 2 = 4" probably will not sink in as fast as showing them the problem, such as giving them two blocks, then adding two more blocks.

Attention. Students with mental retardation may also have difficulty paying attention to appropriate details. For example, suppose that a teacher is teaching students addition facts. For a week, the teacher drills the students by writing "2 + 1", "2 + 2", "2 + 3", etc. across the blackboard. The student with mental retardation might remember that "2 + 1 = 3," but only because it is the first problem that the teacher writes on the board. So, if the teacher were to write "2 + 2" first, the student would answer "3".

In other words, students with mental retardation often do not know the details to which they are suppose to pay attention. When you look at this page, you know to pay attention to how the letters form words, the structure of each sentence, and the type of punctuation used. Students with mental retardation, on the other hand, might pay attention to the color of the type or the size of the page. Consequently, they might have difficulty learning to read.

Generalization. Generalization is a term for the ability to transfer what you learn from one task or in an environment to another. For example, when your parents taught you how to use a telephone, you probably were able to use other phones in other locations, such as at your neighbor's house or at work. Students with mental retardation frequently have difficulty with generalizations. They might learn how to tie their shoes, but when you buy them a new pair, they appear to have forgotten this skill.

Memory. Students with mental retardation also have difficulties with their short-term memory. That is, their ability to recall information that was recently presented to them (e.g., 2 or 3 seconds ago) is diminished. Usually, this is because individuals with mental retardation do not actively process information like most people do. For instance, if you are introduced to somebody for the first time and you want to remember their name, you might repeat it over and over in your head, or you might picture their name in writing. You actively try to learn new information. People with mental retardation do not utilize these types of strategies. As a result, they might have difficulty recalling sequences of tasks that you just told them.

Motivation.   Motivating individuals with mental retardation can often be a troublesome task. Many have experienced failure so frequently that they learn to expect it all the time. Because of these expectations, they may give up easily or not even try. They may even use their mental retardation as an excuse for poor performance or behavior. This is called learned helplessness.

Related to learned helplessness, people with mental retardation also have an external locus of control. That is, they think that they have very little control over how things turn out. For example, a student with mental retardation might believe that they got a perfect on a spelling test because the teacher was in a good mood, rather than because they studied the material longer.

Motivating individuals with mental retardation is also problematic because many lack self-direction. Even when they want to engage in an activity, they may wait for other people to initiate it or help them with the next step. As a result, they develop a dependence on other people, rather than attempting to do things themselves.

Conditions Associated with Mental Retardation

There are many conditions associated with mental retardation. For example, some individuals with mental retardation also have autism or Down's Syndrome. Several of these conditions are discussed briefly below. If you which to learn more about these conditions, please consult the resources listed in Chapter #7.

Autism.   Autism is defined by IDEA as:

> . . . a developmental disability significantly affecting verbal and nonverbal communication and social interaction, generally evident before age 3, that adversely affects educational performance. Other characteristics often associated with autism are engagement in repetitive activities and stereotyped movements, resistance to environmental change or changes in daily routines, and unusual responses to sensory experiences.

Not everybody with autism has mental retardation. In fact, it is very possible that children with autism can be cognitively gifted. Some also are savants and demonstrate dramatic strengths, such as being able to memorize everything they read or being able to do complex mathematical problems.

Down's syndrome.   Down's syndrome is a condition caused by abnormal chromosomal development. Individuals with Down's syndrome tend to have thick epicanthic folds in the corners of their eyes, thick tongues, and short fingers. They also tend to be short in stature, overweight with poor muscle tone, and have hyperflexible joints, and small mouths. It is very common for individuals with Down's syndrome to have heart defects, to develop upper respiratory infections and leukemia, and to have difficulties speaking clearly (usually due to their large tongues and small mouths). While most individuals with Down's syndrome have mild to moderate mental retardation, some have average intelligence.

Fragile X syndrome.   Like Down's syndrome, fragile X syndrome is a hereditary condition that frequently is associated with mental retardation. Basically, fragile X is caused by damage to the X chromosome. Individuals with this condition tend to have:

- big heads
- large, flat ears
- broad noses
- prominent foreheads
- large hands with nontapering fingers
- long, thin faces

Also like individuals with Down's syndrome, students with Fragile X syndrome tend to have various degrees of mental retardation. However, some may have normal intelligence.

William's syndrome.   William's syndrome is another chromosomal-related disorder that can be associated with mental retardation. Individuals with William's syndrome have elf-like facial features, including pointed ears and small faces. While they tend to have deficits in reading, writing, and math, they frequently have extraordinary strengths in spoken language and social skills. Further, they often have heart defects and can be very sensitive to sound. They too can have average intelligence.

Fetal alcohol syndrome (FAS) and fetal alcohol effects (FAE).
When exposed to alcohol prior to birth, many children will be born with
either fetal alcohol syndrome (FAS) or fetal alcohol effects (FAE). Children with FAS typically have:

- Smaller statures for their age
- Flat faces
- Droopy eyelids
- Wide noses
- Small heads
- Heart defects
- Mild to moderate mental retardation

FAE is considered a milder version of FAS. Children with FAE
tend to:

- Be highly distractable
- Have language and cognitive delays
- Poor social skills
- Excessive energy
- Mild mental retardation

LEARNING DISABILITIES

All too often, people misunderstand what learning disabilities are and
how they can manifest themselves. It is incorrectly believed that learning disabilities is a polite way of saying "mild mental retardation."
However, mental retardation and learning disabilities are completely
separate conditions.

Defining Learning Disabilities

When we defined mental retardation, we talked about a student's intelligence being compared to the population as a whole. One of the key
characteristics of mental retardation was to have an IQ score significantly below the average of one's peer group. IQ, however, plays no role
in defining learning disability. Students with learning disabilities can
have any IQ. Further, they frequently are gifted. So what is the definition of learning disabilities?

Discrepancy.   The defining characteristic of learning disabilities is that there is a severe discrepancy between students' aptitude and achievement. That is, they should be doing much better than they are. For example, they might score very high in mathematics but have trouble reading. Or they might have high scores on standardized tests, but are failing most of their classes.

Not other factors.   You can say that individuals with learning disabilities do not live up to their "potential" academically. That is the main criteria for being diagnosed with a learning disability, but it is not the only one. In order to have a learning disability, the discrepancy between aptitude and actual achievement cannot be caused by such factors as a sensory impairment (e.g., they can see the blackboard), mental retardation, or other disabilities. Further, the problem cannot be the result of cultural bias, environmental issues (e.g., background noise), or fatigue.

So let's suppose that a student is very intelligent and should be doing extremely well in her classes, but she isn't. Does that mean she has a learning disability? Such a diagnosis must be determined. It could be that her teachers are not very effective. Or that the classrooms are too noisy. Or that she has problems at home. The possible explanations, other than having a learning disability, are endless.

Types of Learning Disabilities

Many people talk about learning disabilities as if there is only one kind. This is not true. There are many different types of learning disabilities. Each has its own characteristics. Knowing what kind of learning disabilities a student has is the first step in developing effective teaching strategies.

Dyslexia.   Of all the different types of learning disabilities, dyslexia is probably the most widely known. It is characterized by a difficulty in reading. To a dyslexic, letters on this page may appear to change and move. For instance, a "p" might rotate to look like a "d". Or two lines of text might blend together. Consequently, students with dyslexia will not only have difficulty reading, but they will also have problems writing, especially if they are trying to copy letters that they perceive are moving.

Dysgraphia.   Much like dyslexics, students with dysgraphia have problems writing. Both students tend to reverse letters, write words backwards, and have very poor penmanship. The difference between dyslexics and dysgraphics is that dyslexics reverse letters because they see them reversed. Dysgraphics reverse letters because they have poor hand-eye coordination. So, if a dysgraphic wanted to write a "w", his or her hands might not move the way wanted. As a result, he might actually write an "m" or a "3". Further, dysgraphics often confuse their right with their left.

Dyscalculia.   Dyscalculia is a learning disability that affects a person's mathematical abilities. People with dyscalculia have difficulties with reasoning, especially with word problems or making comparisons. People with dyscalculia also have difficulty converting mathematical equations into ordinary language. For example, they might know what 2 + 2 is, but they would have trouble explaining it.

Dysnomia.   Students with learning disabilities can also have problems expressing themselves. For example, have you ever wanted to tell somebody something, but you just couldn't find the words? You know what you want to say, but the words get stuck as if they are on the tip of your tongue. When this happens frequently, students could have what is called dysnomia.

Dysnomia is a learning disability that affects a person's expressive language abilities. They will know a word, such as "car", but they will have difficulty saying it. Don't get this confused with a speech problem, such as stuttering. The person can speak clearly, but they can't seem to say what they want to say. So, instead of saying "car", a dysnomic person might say, "You know . . . that thing. The thing that we drive. It's red. Has a steering wheel. You know what I mean."

Receptive language.   Just as somebody can have problems with their expressive language, they can also have a learning disability that affects their receptive language. People with receptive language learning disabilities, might have difficulty processing information that they hear. For instance, if you tell a student with a receptive language disability your phone number, they might remember the first or last number. Or they might remember all of the numbers, but in the wrong order.

This is not to say that people with receptive language learning disabilities are hard of hearing or are deaf. Nothing is wrong with their hearing. They simply do not learn very effectively through hearing. If you show them your phone number, or have them dial it with their finger, they probably will remember it better.

BEHAVIOR DISORDERS

When people hear the term "behavior disorders", also called emotionally disturbed, they often think of kids who set fires, steal, and disrupt the classroom. However, this in not a complete or accurate picture. As we will discuss, behavior disorders comprise a diverse set of conditions. Understanding the specific condition is essential in teaching students with behavior disorders.

Defining Behavior Disorders

There are many different definitions of behavior disorders. For example, IDEA defines serious emotional disturbance as:

(1) The term ("emotional disturbance") means a condition exhibiting one or more of the following characteristics over a long time and to a marked degree that adversely affects a student's performance.
  (a) an inability to learn, which cannot be explained by intellectual, sensory, and health factors
  (b) an inability to build or maintain satisfactory interpersonal relationships with peers and teachers
  (c) inappropriate types of behavior or feelings under normal circumstances
  (d) a general pervasive mood of unhappiness or depression or
  (e) a tendency to develop physical symptoms or fears associated with personal or school problems

(2) The term includes schizophrenia. The term does not apply to children who are socially maladjusted, unless it is determined that they have an emotional disturbance (Hunt and Marshall, 1999).

The Council for Children with Behavioral Disorders (CCBD) proposed another definition that was later adopted by the National Mental Health and Special Education Coalition (NMHSEC).

(1) Behavioral or emotional responses in school programs so different from appropriate age, cultural, or ethnic norms that they adversely affect educational performance, including academic, social, vocational or personal skills. Such a disability is:

(a) more than a temporary, expected response to stressful events in the environment

(b) consistently exhibited in two different settings, at least one of which is school-related

(c) unresponsive to direct intervention in general education, or the condition of the child is such that general education interventions would be insufficient.

(2) Emotional and behavior disorders can co-exist with other disabilities,

(3) This category may include children or youth with schizophrenic disorders, affective disorders, anxiety disorders, or other sustained disorders of conduct or adjustment when they adversely affect educational performance as described in paragraph (1). (Forness and Knitzer, 1992; McIntyre & Forness, 1996)

These definitions have several components in common:

• The person's behavior is problematic in some way.
• The person's behavior is not caused by another disability, normal response to a situation, or the person's culture.
• The person's behavior is long-lasting and present in multiple environments.

Problematic behavior.   Let's suppose that a student steals something from a store. As we will discuss shortly, stealing is a key characteristic of some behavior disorders. But does that mean the student has a behavior disorder? Well, it depends. Maybe the student didn't mean to steal it. He simply forgot that he had it in his hand as he walked out of the store. Or maybe he had mental retardation and didn't know that stealing was wrong.

Problematic behavior is typically evaluated in two ways:

• Frequency of the behavior
• Intensity of the behavior

If the student's behavior is far more frequent than is traditionally expected, it could be considered problematic. For instance, if the student described above steals once and never does it again, then he probably does not have a behavior disorder. However, if he steals so chronically that he cannot go into a store without taking something, then a diagnosis of a behavior disorder might be appropriate.

The same is true for fire setting. It is not uncommon for a child to have a natural curiosity about fire. So they might play with matches in the backyard from time to time. This could be considered "normal" development. However, if the child frequently sets fires to hurt other people, then the behavior could be seen as problematic.

So what is considered "too frequent"? How many times can a student steal or set fires before he is considered abnormal? Nobody can really say. It is usually up to the IEP team to determine if the frequency is making the behavior problematic and whether the behavior constitutes a disability.

You might be wondering if a student can have problematic behavior that does not occur frequently. The answer is yes. Clearly there are some behaviors, such as rape or murder, which are behaviorally problematic even if they occur only once. In other words, behaviors can be seen as a problem if they are far more intense than is normal.

For instance, suppose that a student is feeling a bit down, but she doesn't feel this way a lot. She could still have a behavior disorder if the feeling is so severe that she wants to kill herself.

The same is true for feelings of anger. We all get angry from time to time. However, if a student gets so angry he or she kills somebody or can't control their actions, a behavior disorder could be the cause.

How intense does a behavior have to be in order to be considered problematic? Again, there is no clear answer. It is very difficult to measure the intensity of depression or anger. The IEP team or behavioral specialist (e.g., counselor, therapist, psychologist) would be responsible for determining whether the behavior is intense.

Unknown cause.   The second component of defining behavior disorders is that the behavior is not caused by another disability, a normal reaction to a stressful situation, or the person's culture. For example, if a student accidentally steals because he has attention deficit disorder and forgot that he had an object in his hand as he left the store, this would not be seen as symptomatic of a behavior disorder. If a student is depressed because her mother just died, a behavior disorder would not be indicated. If a student gets angry quickly because of cultural upbringing, he does not have a behavior disorder. In other words, the cause of the problematic behavior is usually unknown.

Long-lasting and multiple environments.   Let's suppose that a student is angry, verbally abusive, and physically hostile, but only in his math class. Is this a behavior disorder? Probably not. More likely, it is a personality conflict between the student and the teacher.

In order to have a behavior disorder, the student must exhibit the problematic behavior for an extended period of time and in multiple environments. What is an extended period of time? This is hard to say.

Remember the example that we gave earlier about a student who is depressed because her mother died? Certainly, it is natural for a child to grieve over the loss of one of her parents. But let's suppose that the child never gets over this loss. Twenty or thirty years pass and she still is feeling depressed. In this scenario, she could have a behavior disorder. As with the frequency and intensity of behavior, it is usually up to mental health professionals to determine whether a behavior has existed for too long.

Types of Behavior Disorders

There are numerous types of behavior disorders. Knowing the specific type helps teachers and parents treat the student. For example, if a student has depression (a type of behavior disorder), counseling and various medications might be beneficial. However, a student with a conduct disorder might require behavior modification. In other words, getting the appropriate help often depends on identifying the specific problem. Labeling a child with a generic behavior disorder doesn't provide much useful information.

Below we will discuss several of the common behavior disorders. There are many more. If you want additional information, please consult the resources presented in Chapter #7 or the latest edition of the *Diagnostic and Statistical Manual of Mental Disorders (DSM),* which is updated frequently by the American Psychiatric Association (APA).

Conduct disorder.   According to the DSM (Fourth Text Revision), the diagnosis criteria for conduct disorder include:

> I. A reoccurring pattern of behavior that violates societal norms or the basic rights of others. Must have three or more of the following criteria during the past 12 months, with at least one criterion being present during the past 6 months.
>> A. Aggression to people or animals
>>> 1. often bullies, threatens, or intimidates others
>>> 2. often starts physical fights

      3. uses weapons against others
      4. physically cruel to people
      5. physically cruel to animals
      6. steals directly from people (e.g., muggings)
      7. rape

  B. Destruction of property
      1. sets fires to damage property
      2. deliberately destroys property by means other than fire setting

  C. Deceitfulness or theft
      1. breaks into other people's homes or cars
      2. frequently lies
      3. steals indirectly from people (e.g., shoplifting)

  D. Serious violation of rules
      1. violates parental curfews
      2. runs away from home
      3. frequently truant from school

II. The inappropriate behavior causes significant social, academic, or occupational problems.

III. The behavior is not caused by any other disabilities (e.g., schizophrenia). (American Psychiatric Association, 2000)

Oppositional Defiant Disorder.   Oppositional Defiant Disorder (ODD) is very much like Conduct Disorder. In fact, they often exhibit similar characteristics and behaviors. However the behaviors associated with ODD tend to be focused on figures of authority and are less severe than those typical of individuals with Conduct Disorder.

The *DSM* (Fourth Text Revision) defines Oppositional Defiant Disorder as:

I. A pattern of defiant behavior, including four or more of the following, lasting for at least six months and is more frequent or severe than typically expected from age or culture group:
  A. loses temper
  B. argues with adults
  C. violates rules
  D. annoys people deliberately
  E. blames others for own problems

F. is easily annoyed by others
G. is angry
H. is malicious

II. The behavior causes significant problems with academic, social, or occupational functioning.
IV. Not caused by other disabilities (e.g., Conduct Disorder) (American Psychiatric Association, 2000).

Depression.   Depression is one of the most common disabilities that individuals experience. Moreover, people with other disabilities (e.g., learning disabilities) suffer from higher rates of severe depression than other segments of the population. There are numerous definitions of various forms of depression. As a general rule, individuals with depression usually display five or more of the following symptoms over at least a two-week period:

- Feelings of sadness or emptiness
- Diminished interest in activities that once produced pleasure
- Significant and unexplained weight change
- Unexplained change in sleep patterns
- Unexplained change in energy level
- Diminished ability to concentrate
- Inappropriate feelings of guilt or worthlessness
- Reoccurring thoughts of death

It should be noted that these characteristics represent a change in somebody's personality and are not caused by an appropriate response to an unpleasant or tragic event (e.g., death in the family). Boxed Discussion 5.1 examines how to spot students who are at-risk of killing themselves.

Schizophrenia.   The term schizophrenia often scares people. People usually associate schizophrenics with dangerous murders and multiple personalities. However, schizophrenia has nothing to do with multiple personalities, and schizophrenics are not necessarily violent. Schizophrenia is characterized by periods of:

- Hallucinations
- Delusions

Boxed Discussion 5.1:   Identifying Students At-Risk of Committing Suicide

Unfortunately, suicide is a reality for many people. When students have behavior disorders, especially depression, the risk of suicide increases dramatically. Below are some common warning signs the people who are considering suicide often exhibit. If you believe that somebody is considering killing themselves, get help immediately. Some of the resources presented in Chapter 7 may be of help.

- Change in personality
- Change in appearance
- Becomes withdrawn
- Gives away once prized items
- Brings up death
- Complaints of physical symptoms
- Academic failure
- Drug and alcohol abuse
- Suddenly seems fine or happy after a prolonged period of depression

---

- Distorted perception of reality
- Inability to experience pleasure

ATTENTION DEFICIT HYPERACTIVITY DISORDERS

Over the past decade, Attention Deficit Hyperactivity Disorder, or ADHD, has become a very popular topic in the national media. Unfortunately, few people truly understand this group of conditions. In this section, we will briefly discuss what ADHD is as well as outline the sub-types of ADHD. If you would like more information about these conditions, you might want to consult some of the resources listed in Chapter #7.

Defining Attention Deficit Hyperactivity Disorders

The definition of ADHD has changed considerably since the 1990s. Perhaps you have heard the term ADD or Attention Deficit Disorder. Technically, ADD is no longer a valid diagnosis. You see, in 1994 the American Psychiatric Association (APA) dropped the term ADD and then broke ADHD (Attention Deficit Hyperactivity Disorder) into four separate categories. The diagnostic criteria for each of these four categories of ADHD are discussed below.

Types of Attention Deficit Hyperactivity Disorders

Unknown to most parents and professionals, there are several sub-types of ADHD. Specifically, there is:

- Attention Deficit Hyperactivity Disorder—Predominantly Inattentive (ADHD-I)
- Attention Deficit Hyperactivity Disorder—Predominantly Hyperactive/Impulsive (ADHD-HI)
- Attention Deficit Hyperactivity Disorder—Combined (ADHD-C)
- Attention Deficit Hyperactivity Disorder—Not Otherwise Specified (ADHD-NOS)

In addition to having the characteristics described in the following sections, other conditions must also be satisfied for somebody to have ADHD, including:

- Some characteristics present before age seven
- Behavior impairs functioning
- Behavior is present in multiple environments
- Not caused by environmental factors, drug use, or any other disability

Attention deficit hyperactive disorder—inattentive. To have ADHD-I, individuals must have six or more of the following characteristics for at least six months to the extent that the behavior is inconsistent with the person's age:

- Frequently makes careless mistakes
- Frequently has difficulty paying attention
- Frequently does not appear to listen when spoken to
- Frequently does not follow through on tasks
- Frequently has difficulty with organization
- Frequently avoids activities that require prolonged mental effort
- Frequently loses things
- Frequently is distracted
- Frequently is forgetful

Attention deficit hyperactive disorder—hyperactive/impulsive. To have ADHD-HI, individuals must have six or more of the following characteristics for at least six months to the extent that the behavior is inconsistent with the person's age:

- Frequently fidgets
- Frequently leaves seat at inappropriate times

- Frequently runs or climbs at inappropriate times
- Frequently has difficulty being quiet
- Frequently has excess energy
- Frequently talks excessively
- Frequently blurts out answers before questions have been completed
- Frequently has difficult waiting turn
- Frequently interrupts

Attention deficit hyperactivity disorder—combined.   If your child meets the criteria for both ADHD-I and ADHD-HI, he would then qualify for ADHD-C.

Attention deficit hyperactivity disorder—not otherwise specified. Let's suppose that your child only has four or five of the characteristics of a type of ADHD, but her functioning is clearly impaired. For example, she would walk in front of a moving car because she doesn't pay attention to what is happening around her. In such a situation, she could be diagnosed with ADHD-NOS, or what use to be called pseudo-ADHD. Table 5.2 provides an estimate for the prevalence of ADHD & other conditions.

Table 5.2.   Estimates of the Prevalence of Various Conditions

Condition	Percent of Population
ADHD	5%
Anorexia	1%
Autism	0.05%
Bi-Polar	1.5%
Bulimia	3%
Conduct Disorders	8%
Depression	15%
Epilepsy	0.5%
Gifted	2%
Hearing Impairment	9%
Learning Disabilities	5%
Mental Retardation	2%
Obsessive Compulsive Disorder	2.5%
Oppositional Defiant Disorder	12%
Paralysis	1%
Schizophrenia	1.5%
Speech Impairments	1%
Stuttering	1%
Tourette's Syndrome	0.3%
Traumatic Brain Injuries	3%
Vision Impairments	3%

Note: These are very rough estimates of the prevalence within the United States. Nobody can say for sure how common each condition is due to differing definitions and methods of obtaining data.
Sources: American Psychiatric Association (2000); Barkley (2000); Fombonne (1999); Hallahan and Kauffman (2000); National Center for Health Statistics (2002); Piirto (1999)

APPLYING WHAT YOU HAVE LEARNED

Go back and review the case study at the beginning of the chapter. Reflect on what has been covered in the chapter and try to answer the questions after the case study. What did you learn?

Question #1: Does Mary Have Mental Retardation

So what do you think? Does Mary have mental retardation? Let's examine the evidence provided in the case study.

Dr. Hernandez gave Mary multiple IQ tests. Each of them found that her IQ averaged around 118. So does she have mental retardation? No. One of the defining characteristics of mental retardation is a sub-average IQ. Mary actually has a higher IQ than most people. Consequently, she could not have mental retardation.

Question #2: Does Mary Have A Behavior Disorder?

The answer to this question is a littler harder to discern. As we discussed earlier, there are many different kinds of behavior disorders. Some, such as conduct disorders, involve clearly inappropriate behaviors. Others, such as depression, are more subtle and harder to recognize. Given the information provided in the case study, does Mary have a behavior disorder? And if so, what type? What do you think?

Dr. Hernandez not only observed Mary in multiple environments, but he also got data from several different teachers. From the information that he gathered, it doesn't appear that Mary has a behavior disorder. Specifically, she is not misbehaving nor does she seem depressed—other than simply being discouraged about her grades. However, depression is a problem that many people with disabilities develop later on in life, so it would be wise if Mary's parents and teachers kept an eye on her.

Question #3: Does Mary Have An Attention Deficit Hyperactive Disorder?

As we discussed in this chapter, ADHD is a very common disability that involves inattention, hyperactivity, and impulsivity. So do you think that Mary has an ADHD? Let's take a look at the facts.

In the case study, Dr. Hernandez specifically indicates that Mary seems to pay attention in class. Further, there is no indication that she has problems being overly active or being impulsive. Moreover, it would be strange for somebody with ADHD to just have problems in one subject area, such as mathematics. Given this information, it would appear that Mary would not have any type of ADHD.

Question #4: Does Mary Have A Learning Disability?

Learning disabilities are very common. In fact, as we mentioned in Chapter 1, many famous people have learning disabilities, such as Tom Cruise. So does Mary have a learning disability? What do you think?

Certainly, it is difficult to diagnose a student based upon the information provided in the case study, but there are several clues that might suggest that Mary has a learning disability. First, there is a discrepancy between what she should be doing verses what she is doing. Specifically, she is obviously very bright, but she is doing poorly in math. Secondly, there is no other apparent explanation for her performance. She tries hard, pays attention, and does well in other classes.

If Mary does have a learning disability, what kind would she have? She probably wouldn't have dyslexia since her reading scores are pretty high. She probably doesn't have an expressive or receptive language learning disability since nobody has complained about her communication skills. The only area that she has difficulty in is math, which could mean that she has a mathematical learning disability or dyscalculia.

CHAPTER 6

Collaboration and Team Building

CHAPTER OBJECTIVES:

By the end of this chapter, you should be able to:

1. Define "team."
2. List various types of teams that teachers will be on.
3. Compare and contrast the roles people play as team members.
4. Identify factors that help teams become effective.
5. Develop ways of improving skills as a team member.

CASE STUDY: COLLABORATING WITH THE USSAKS

"I would like to welcome everybody to Sally's annual IEP meeting," Mrs. Denver, Sally's special education teacher, began. "Our task today is to re-evaluate Sally's status in general education and to determine whether or not there is a more appropriate placement for her." Mrs. Denver turned to Sally's parents, Mr. and Mrs. Ussak. "Before we get underway, do you have any questions?" There was a long, awkward silence as the Ussaks said and did nothing.

"I want to say something," Mr. Pelleck suddenly interjected in a rather loud voice. "Sally isn't doing very well in my class. She is finally turning in assignments, but they are almost always late. Plus, she hasn't done well on any of the tests. I really don't think that she is smart enough to be in regular education. And oh! She will speak to her friends in the hallway, but she never seems to say anything during class! It is as if she is going out of her way to ignore me."

"You should consider that a blessing, considering your other students!" Mr. Matte said, getting a nervous laugh from everybody but the Ussaks.

"It is not that I don't like Sally," Mr. Pelleck continued looking at the Ussaks briefly. "I am sure she is a nice kid in some way, but she is not exactly the sharpest knife in the drawer, if you know what I mean. She isn't what I would call bright. She doesn't belong in regular education."

"Well, uh mm," Mrs. Denver stammered apprehensively. "Thank you for . . . um . . . sharing your thoughts, Mr. Pelleck. Perhaps, some of Sally's other teachers might tell us what they think."

"She is shy," Miss McAfee admitted, "however, I think she is better served in regular. . . ."

"No," Mr. Pelleck interrupted shaking his head, "Don't give me that crap. You are going to tell me that it's 'better to put her in regular education so that she can learn social skills.'" He said in a voice mocking Miss McAfee's. "I say, at what expense? What about all of the other kids? They have a right to a free and appropriate education too—even thought they aren't disabled."

"Mr. Horwitz," Mrs. Denver said tentatively as she turned away from Mr. Pelleck to face Sally's English teacher. "What do you think? How is Sally doing in your class?"

"He thinks the same as me," Mr. Pelleck responded sharply. "Retarded kids don't belong in our classes. Trust me, I have worked in this school district for twenty-three years. I know that this inclusion thing won't work. Every year it is the same thing. Some administrator or lawmaker thinks that it is such a hot idea to push handicapped kids on regular education teachers even though it never works. They are a distraction to the other kids and take up too much of our time. Sally, and kids like her, should be in special rooms most, if not all, of the day. In Sally's case, I would be willing to have her attend gym or art with the normal kids. I am sure she can socialize there."

All through this discussion, the Ussaks said and did nothing as they have for every IEP meeting they have ever attended.

CASE STUDY QUESTIONS

After completing this chapter, you should be able to answer the following questions:

1. Why might Mr. and Mrs. Ussaks not be participating?
2. How could you get the family to participate more?
3. What roles did Mr. Pelleck play in the meeting?
4. How could this team be more effective?

INTRODUCTION

As we have discussed throughout this entire book, effective education for students with disabilities often hinges upon developing effective educational planning. Developing effective education plans requires input from multiple sources with diverse perspectives, including the student, teachers, and family members. Thus, in order to help prepare students with disabilities for their futures, these individuals must act like a team.

However, when team members have such diverse perspectives and expectations, conflict can often arise. The purpose of this chapter is to discuss the team building process. It also presents ways to make teams collaborate more effectively, especially when team members don't see eye-to-eye.

In this chapter we will discuss:

- The definition of "team"
- How teams develop
- The roles the team members play
- Ways parents can build effective teams
- What to do if trouble starts

DEFINING "TEAM"

Perhaps the best way to begin is by asking, "What is a team?" This probably sounds like a simple question, but it really isn't. Think about it. Is a team simply a group of people? Or is it something more? According to Johnson and Johnson (1997), a team is ". . . a set of interpersonal relationships structured to achieve established goals" (p. 570). A team, therefore, is more than a group of people who randomly or accidentally get together. Specifically, researchers have identified several key characteristics that define "teams" (Friend & Cook, 2000; Scholtes, Joiner, & Streibel, 1996). Each of these is discussed in the subsequent pages and summarized in Table 6.1.

Awareness of Being A Team Member

In order to be an effective team, members must realize that they are associated with each other. Further, teammates are connected by a set of shared believes. For example, they have to believe that what they are

Table 6.1. Summary of Team Components

Component	Description
Team Awareness	Members must be aware that they are part of the team.
Interactions	Members must interact.
Interdependence	The work of each team member affects the team as a whole.
Roles	Members play specific roles.
Goal	The team is trying to accomplish a mutually understood goal.

doing is important or worthwhile. Without members being aware that they are on a team and having similar beliefs as other members, effective teams cannot exist.

Interactions Between Team Members

Not only must team members realize that they are a part of a team, they must also interact with each other over time. After all, it would be difficult to work effectively if each team member did not have some sort of contact with each other. Imagine being at an IEP meeting where only the special education teacher talked. That isn't a team. It is a presentation.

This does not mean that teams have to be face-to-face. In fact, nowadays, thanks to e-mails and teleconferences, it is very easy to work with people who are half way around the world. Still, teams must exchange ideas and information in order to achieve their purpose.

Interdependence of Team Members

Interdependence of team members means that what affects one team member, affects the team as a whole. For example, suppose that each member of an IEP team were given an assignment. Further, each of the assignments needs to be completed in order for the team to accomplish its mission. If one team member does not complete his or her assignment, the entire team will suffer because their purpose will not be achieved. In other words, there is individual accountability within teams.

Members Have Specific Roles

Another characteristic of a team is that each member has specific roles to play. For example, some people tend to lead discussions while others like to assume the role of "devil's advocate." When a member doesn't have a role to play, they cease to be a participating member of the team. Another potential problem with team roles is that sometimes various roles conflict. When this happens, teams may become ineffective. Later in this chapter, the roles that team members often play will be discussed as well as how to address situations where team members have taken on counterproductive roles (e.g., "the Dominator").

Addressing A Common Goal

Perhaps the most important characteristic of a team is that it shares a common goal. Again, this might sound obvious; however, all too often IEP meetings deteriorate into an argument between various team members. These arguments can frequently be avoided if team members remember that they are each there for the same reason—to help a student with disabilities succeed. Without having a goal, these teams become nothing more than social gatherings.

THE DEVELOPMENT OF TEAMS

Effective teams do not just suddenly spring out of nothingness. Teams develop through a series of stages (Bennis & Shepard; 1956; Tuckman and Jensen, 1977). Further, team members have different needs during each of these stage. By understanding how teams develop, you can help your child's IEP team develop into a productive unit focusing upon the same outcome—helping your child. Table 6.2 summarizes the stages of team development.

Stage 1: Forming

Obviously the first stage a team goes through involves its formation (i.e., forming). This is the period where somebody determines that a team needs to be developed to accomplish a specific goal. For example, you might think that your child has a disability, so you ask your child's teachers to get together to discuss your concerns.

During this stage, team members introduce themselves to each other, learn of their task, and clarify the function of the team. Don't expect a lot to get done during this stage. People need to understand why they are getting together before they can be productive.

Table 6.2. Summary of Team Development Stages

Stage	Description
Forming	The team is just getting together to learn its purpose.
Storming	Team members are trying to find their roles.
Norming	Team members have identified their roles and are coming together as a team.
Performing	The team is being productive and moving toward accomplishing its goal.
Adjourning	The team dissolves.

Stage 2: Storming

Once a team is formed, members could experience a period where issues relating to team roles and procedures are addressed (i.e., the storming stage). This is frequently a time of unrest as members attempt to understand each other, as well as interpret the task at hand. During this period, considerable arguing might take place, since no dominant leader has emerged.

For example, suppose that you ask all of your child's teachers to get together. You have everybody introduce themselves and then explain why everybody is there—or what the team's goal is (e.g., to find out if your child has a disability). During the storming stage, team members will attempt to define their roles in the process. Some people might try to take over the leadership role or guide the team into addressing unrelated topics.

Stage 3: Norming

Once the turmoil of the storming stage has subsided, teams might go through the norming stage. A clear leader emerges and cliques within the team are formed. During this stage, the team also determines how they will undertake their task.

Various team members might be assigned certain tasks. For example, the special educator might offer to observe your child in order to determine why she is having a problem in class. The school psychologist might offer to conduct standardized tests in an effort to learn your child's strengths and weaknesses. Or you might offer to bring your child into a pediatrician to see if there are any medical explanations for your concerns.

Stage 4: Performing

With everybody's roles delineated, the actual act of trying to accomplis the team's goal takes place. This occurs in the performing stage.

During the course of their "lives," teams may frequently regress from the performing stage to previous stages. For example, you might find yourself in an IEP meeting where everybody is being productive, but every so often a team member might attempt to gain control or get the team off course.

Stage 5: Adjourning

No team lives forever. At some point teams dissolve, whether they were successful or not. However, it is likely that a new team will emerge later on with a similar goal. Thus, adjourning doesn't necessarily mean "the end." It may simply mean a change in team members, roles, or goals.

ROLES OF TEAM MEMBERS

Much like good books or television shows, teams tend to have several different characters who each play different roles. Some of these roles are helpful. Others are counter-productive. Recognizing each role will help you make your team more effective.

Team roles can be divided into three categories:

- Group Task,
- Group Building and Maintenance, and
- Self-Centered roles.

Each of these categories contains several diverse, as well as overlapping, roles. Moreover, people might exhibit the characteristics of several roles at one time or during the course of the same interaction.

Group Task Roles

Group task roles involve behaviors related to achieving the team's goal (see Table 6.3). For example, one of the purposes of IEP teams is to determine the most appropriate placement for a student. Any behaviors directed to that end involve group task roles. On the other hand, when IEP team members are just chitchatting with each other during a break, this would not be a group task role since it had nothing to do with the student's IEP. Below are brief discussions regarding several group

Table 6.3.   Summary of Group Task Roles

Role	Characteristics
Coordinator	Brings together several pieces of information
Elaborator	Further clarifies or explains the ideas of other members
Energizer	Motivates other team members
Evaluator-Critic	Judges the information being presented
Information Giver	Presents relevant information
Information Seeker	Requests for clarification or additional data
Initiator-Contributor	Offers new ideas
Opinion Giver	Shares own opinions
Opinion Seeker	Attempts to obtain other members' perceptions
Orienter	Keeps discussion on-task
Procedural Technician	Hands the technical aspect of holding a meeting
Recorder	Keeps track of the team's progress

task roles. Remember that people may exhibit several of these roles during the same interaction or meeting.

Coordinator.   Coordinators synthesize information (fact or opinion) from different group members. They might also be in charge of running the meeting. Coordinators might say something like "The test results presented by Bill, and the teacher evaluations that Mary just shared with us, seem to indicate that the behavior modification program is working."

Elaborator.   Elaborators explain information, such as data presented by the Information Giver (discussed in another section). Elaborators attempt to make sure everybody is on the same page. For example, they might say something like, "In other words, Yolanda's test results indicate that she is at age-appropriate levels for science and math, but not for reading."

Energizer.   Energizers are the team members who motivate the group into beginning a task or remaining on-task. These people are often considered the "cheerleaders" of the team. When the team is getting tired or having trouble starting, Energizers frequently try to increase everybody's morale. They might say something like, "Okay, we are almost done. We are doing a great job! Let's hang in there and finish this last section of the IEP!"

Evaluator-critic.   Evaluator-critics assess the progress of the group or information presented. They might seem overly critical at times when in fact they are just pointing out potential flaws in people's plans or information. They might say something like, "We could use the mornings to give Sally community-based instruction, but the fact is, we just don't have the staffing to do so."

Information giver.   Information Givers offer neutral information, or facts, to be considered by the rest of the group. They are not necessarily presenting their own opinion of what should be done. Rather, they are simply stating information for everybody to evaluate. They might say something like, "After we started the new reinforcement program, Huey didn't miss a day of school."

Information seeker.   Information Seekers request clarification of ideas. They might also ask for data related to the topic at hand, such as evidence demonstrating that a student completed last year's IEP goals. They might ask a question like, "Do we know for sure that the administration will not allow Sarah to be taught within the community?"

Initiator-contributor.   Initiator-contributors suggest new ideas or restate old ideas in a new way. For example, if the meeting is going nowhere, the Initiator will try to jump-start the proceedings by offering a new direction. They might ask something like, "If we can't bring the student to the community, how about if we bring the community to the student?"

Opinion giver.   Opinion Givers present their own opinions about the topic at hand. Their perceptions do not have to be requested by other team members. Opinion Givers may simply state how they feel. For example, they might say "I don't know about all of you, but I think this is great news."

Opinion seeker.   Opinion Seekers attempt to determine what other people think about the topic at hand. Opinion Seekers might also try to get other people involved by asking them questions. Or they might attempt to see if there is a consensus within the group. They might ask something like, "What do you think about the results of these tests?"

Orienter.   Orienters guide the group back on track when they have gotten off-task. They also help prevent unneeded slowdowns, such as when the group reaches a sticking point on a tough topic. Orienters might say something like, "Let's keep in mind why we are here. We need to figure out what skills Toby needs to learn to be able to succeed in the third grade."

Procedural technician.   Procedural Technicians take care of routine matters so that the meeting can be conducted. For example, they might make copies of needed documents, reserve the meeting space, or rearrange the room to match the needs of the group. A Procedural Technician might say something like, "We are going to need these new IEP forms so I made extra copies."

Recorder.   Recorders monitor the group's progress, perhaps by taking notes. They usually have a good grasp of what has happened historically with the group. For example, they might say, "According to last meeting's notes, we decided to forego that discussion until next school year."

Group Building and Maintenance Roles

Whereas Group Task roles involve the completion of the team's goals, Group Building and Maintenance roles involve maintaining constructive interpersonal relations within the group (see Table 6.4). For example, suppose that two or more team members do not get along. Non-task-related interactions between these individuals may fall into this category. As with Group Task roles, individuals can perform multiple Group Building and Maintenance roles during the same meeting.

Compromiser.   Compromisers try to generate ideas that bring together different "camps" within the group. For example, if half of the team holds one position and the other half believes something different, Compromisers will attempt to create a solution so that all members will be satisfied. They might say something like, "How about if we do a little of what everybody is saying. Maybe we could include Paul in regular education classes during the mornings and in Voc-tech classes in the afternoon?"

Encourager.   Encouragers try to support group members. They might be considered the emotional leaders of the team. If they think somebody is feeling down, Encouragers will attempt to make them feel better. They might say something supportive like, "You did a great job with that report! It must have taken you a lot of effort."

Follower.   Followers are team members who go along with the majority. Even if they might disagree, they will support whatever idea is

Table 6.4.   Summary of Group Building and Maintenance Roles

Role	Characteristics
Compromiser	Comes up with ideas to please everybody
Encourager	Emotionally supports other team members
Follower	Goes along with the majority of the team
Gatekeeper	Promotes participation
Group Observer	Assesses the mood of the team
Harmonizer	Defuses conflict between team members
Standard Keeper	Holds the team to a specified level of performance

held by rest of the group. They might say something like, "If everybody else likes how these goals are written, I will agree to sign the IEP."

Gatekeeper.   Gatekeepers try to give everyone opportunities to be involved. If somebody seems to be too shy to state an opinion, Gatekeepers might ask the persona question or encourage him or her to share ideas. They might say something like "It looked as if you had an opinion about that Mrs. Tucker. What do you think about all of this?"

Group observer.   Group Observers evaluate the group's status. They might notice if time is running out or whether people are getting frustrated. They might say something like, "I think that everybody wants to table this discussion and skip ahead to the evaluation report."

Harmonizer.   Harmonizers defuse conflicts between group members. When personal conflicts begin to surface, Harmonizers will attempt to break the tension, often by using humor or redirection. They might say something like, "If we stay in this meeting any longer, they are going to start charging us rent."

Standard keeper.   Standard Keepers set criterion for the group to achieve. These standards could be related to the actual agenda or expected conduct, such as dress code or use of Robert's Rules of Order. A Standard Keeper might say something like, "We are scheduled to get done with this project by next week. We will need to be more on-task if we are going to reach that deadline."

Self-Centered Roles

The final group of roles that team members perform is called self-centered roles (see Table 6.5). These roles focus upon satisfying an

Table 6.5.   Summary of Self-Centered Roles

Role	Characteristics
Aggressor	Attacks the ideas or character of other team members
Blocker	Prevents ideas from getting considered or supported by other team members
Dominator	Dominates the discussion
Help Seeker	Obtains help from other people in an attempt to decrease the amount of work needing to be accomplished
Player	Plays around rather than be on-task
Recognition Seeker	Frequently cites own work in an effort to increase status within group
Self-Confessor	Discusses personal problems rather than be on-task
Special Interest Pleader	Advocates for own interests

individual's needs rather than the needs of the group. For example, a team member may feel strongly about a certain employment option (e.g., sheltered workshops). As a result, the person's bias might influence whether students are referred to those programs. As with other roles, people may not be aware that they are fulfilling a self-centered role. This is why self-reflection is so important to being a successful team member.

Aggressor.   Aggressors are team members who attempt to improve their own standing by belittling another member's idea or character. They are often defensive and quick to anger. They might be considered the "team bully." Aggressors might say something like, "Well, that is a worthless suggestion."

Blocker.   Blockers prevent opposing ideas from gaining support. They frequently refuse to act as a member of the group. They might say something like, "No. That won't work. I don't even want to waste my time considering that idea."

Dominator.   Dominators monopolize the attention and time of the group. They typically do this with long-winded monologues that add little value to the group process. For example, they might say something like, "I think this troublesome problem can be broken into fifteen different and very separate points. Number one, which is only slightly more important than number two which I will talk about shortly. . . ."

Help seeker.   Help Seekers frequently attempt to gain assistance for other group members. They typically do this when they do not wish to do an assigned task. For example, they might explain how they are inadequate for the task. They might say something like, "Jim is much better at conducting in-home assessments than I am. He should do it, not me."

Players.   Players[1] get the group off-task by initiating inappropriate play. In other words, they might be the people in a team who are always "goofing off." They might say something like, "Here's my imitation of Mel Gibson."

Recognition seeker.   Recognition Seekers see themselves as experts and often try to dominate the conversation or try to control the decision-making process. To support their positions and sense of superiority, they will brag about past accomplishments and overstate their abilities.

---

[1] The term "Playboy" was used by Tuckman (1965) to define this role. This term can be interpreted as a sexist comment since women can fulfill this role as well as men. Thus, we prefer the term "Player" and have chosen to use it in this text.

For example, they might say something like, "Trust me, I have done this a million times. I know what to do here."

 Self-confessor.   Like Players, Self-Confessors will get the team off-topic by bringing up personal feelings that are unrelated to the task at hand. These feelings are likely to be negative or distracting to the rest of the team. They might say something like, "I am sorry that I can't concentrate on this stuff. I am having a horrible time with my teenage daughter. She is going out with the wrong guys, and I just don't know what to do."

Special-interest pleader.   Special-interest pleaders attach non-scheduled issues to the discussion. They often advocate for certain ideas because acceptance of the ideas helps them personally. They might say something like, "I think that we should change the special education curriculum for the entire district. In fact, I think we should adopt the book that I wrote last summer."

HOW PARENTS CAN BUILD EFFECTIVE TEAMS

As a parent, you have a great deal of impact on the effectiveness of your child's IEP team. You can either sit back and let the "professionals" handle your child's future (which I hope you won't do) or you can become active and equal members of the team. Below are ways that you can make your child's IEP team run more effectively.

Fostering Individual Accountability

Imagine being part of a team where one person did absolutely nothing, but later took most of the credit for what everybody else did. In those situations, there was little individual accountability. Nobody knew who did what and nobody got the appropriate amount of credit.

Individual accountability is important because it motivates everybody to participate, as well as do their best work. Further, individual accountability allows the rest of the team to evaluate the strengths and limitations of team members. Without understanding team members' strengths and limitations, it is difficult to cultivate an effective team.

Making Interdependence Positive

Positive interdependence is where everybody benefits from being part of the team. Consider, for example, a quarterback on a football team. In order for the quarterback to have a good game (i.e., high rate of completions), the receivers must also have to have a good game (i.e., high rate of receptions). All teams need to have this kind of "win-win" relationship. In other words, team members have to change the mindset from "me" to "we." Later in this chapter, strategies for creating this mindset will be discussed.

Developing Plans

Effective teams have plans. How exactly are members going to approach the team's goal? What will they focus on first? Who is going to do what? How are members going to evaluate whether their approach is working? These are only a few questions that teams may need to address.

To develop a plan of attack, team members first might want to examine the goal and break it into smaller, more manageable, tasks. Then perhaps divide the team into work groups and assign tasks to groups that have the required expertise. Don't forget to think about the resources that the team will need to accomplish each task (e.g., computer programs, flip charts and markers, secretarial assistance, etc.). Finally, develop timelines, but realize that nothing is ever set in stone. The best-made plans are flexible, realistic, and not overwhelming.

Utilizing Expertise

There is an old expression "You can't make omelets without eggs." Likewise, it is difficult to develop effective IEPs without team members who have the appropriate skills and knowledge. For example, let's suppose that your child has Attention Deficit Hyperactivity Disorder—Combined (ADHD-C). If nobody on the team understands ADHDs, developing an effective IEP will be problematic. It would be like trying to conduct complicated surgery with a spoon, butter knife, and frying pan.

Sometimes, teams may need to recruit additional team members who have the needed expertise. Or teams could solicit advice from outside experts. More importantly, teams will need to understand the skills and knowledge already held by teammates. It may be that they already have what the team needs. Later in this chapter, ways of getting to know teammates will be discussed.

Establishing Ground Rules

Imagine an IEP team where nobody really knew what was going on. Nobody knew who the leader was or what forms to fill out or in what order tasks should be done. This would not be an effective team. It would be much like when kids try to play a game and none of them knew the rules. A lot of squabbling is likely to take place.

To efficiently achieve the team's goals, everybody has to understand the team's operating procedures. For example, when the meeting is said to start at 8:00, does that mean that there will be fifteen minutes of socializing first? Do you have to raise your hand if you want to share a thought? Does the team follow formal rules of order? Before a team can be effective, every member must be aware of how the team is going to be run. Spending the first few minutes of each meeting reminding everybody of the team's procedures might help people stay on track. Table 6.6 outlines suggestions for running good meetings.

Well-Balanced Participation

One of the advantages to teams is that they have a wealth of knowledge, skills, and perspectives. If only one person participates in a team, it wouldn't be a team at all. That one person might as well hold meetings by himself. In order to harness the power of teams, everybody has to participate. Further, team members should participate as equally as possible. Later in this chapter, methods for dealing with dominating team members, as well as how to get shy members to participate more, will be discussed.

Table 6.6.   Guidelines for Good Meetings

- Have a clear agenda (include topics of conversation, people responsible for reports, estimated time needed)
- Send the agenda to team members prior to the meeting
- Review the purpose of the meeting before and during the meeting
- Have all of the need materials on hand
- Have extra copies of materials that will be, and have been, handed out
- Insure the room is conducive to holding a meeting (e.g., enough space, chairs, tables, not to warm or cold, etc.)
- If the meeting is lengthy, vary the method of presentation (e.g., take breaks and allow people to review material, use small and large group activities, etc.)
- Make sure everybody knows each other (e.g., have introduction, name plates, etc.)
- Summarize the results of the meeting before everybody leaves
- Make sure everybody understands their tasks, if tasks are assigned
- Send minutes of the meeting to team members

Make Goals Clear, Important, and Obtainable

Imagine that developing your child's IEP involves many complicated issues (e.g., identifying communication devices, developing behavior modification plans, monitoring health-related concerns). So the IEP team separates into workgroups, each brainstorming potential answers for a particular issue. Unfortunately, each workgroup spends most of the allotted time asking each other "What are we supposed to do?" If teams do not know what they are supposed to do, a great deal of time can be wasted.

In order for a team to be effective, every team member must have a clear understanding of the team's goals. Further, everybody's understanding has to be the same. Just imagine the chaos in a group when half the members thought that they were suppose to accomplish one goal while the other half of the members were trying to accomplish a totally different goal!

In order to help everybody to be on the same page, goals should be concise. The more convoluted the goal, the more likely people will become confused. This is much like having driving directions that are unclear and go on for many pages. People are likely to get lost. Further, goals should have an obvious, measurable outcome. That is, everybody on the team should know when the team's purpose has been fulfilled.

Finally, imagine going to a meeting with your child's teachers. They are all excited about something or other, but you just don't see the point. To make teams effective, everybody needs to understand the importance of the team's goal. It is really hard for team members to become motivated about tasks that they feel are unnecessary or counterproductive. Later in this chapter, ways of building teams so that everybody understands the importance of the team's goal will be discussed.

Understanding Other Professionals

Many of the problems that multidisciplinary teams experience stem from a lack of understanding of other people's jobs. As we discussed in Chapter 1, not all educators have the same background and training. Even some of the core philosophies are different. Consequently, teachers and parents tend to see students in very different lights.

In order to prevent misunderstandings, team members will need to educate each other about their jobs and perspectives. For instance, during the formation stage, have people introduce themselves and talk about their jobs. Have them explain what it is like to be a social studies teacher or an early childhood specialist. Have them discuss what they like about their jobs and what they don't like about their jobs. A lot of people might not realize what it is like to be in a different field. Not all educators have the same job!

How Can I Be A Better Team Member?

In order to have a successful team, team members must be effective at their roles. But how can people be better team members? Below are some problems that teams often experience, as well as several strategies that might help them overcome each problem.

Improving Listening Skills

Ineffective team members often have poor listening skills. This is not to say that they have a hearing impairment. It is just that they do not always attend to, understand, or recall appropriate information at the appropriate time. Without these skills, it is hard to be an effective team member (see Table 6.7). So how can team members become better listeners? First, understand what causes poor listening.

Outside distractions.   Imagine trying to listen to somebody at a party. There is loud music, people saying hello from across the room, movement all around. Distractions take attention away from the speaker. In situations where outside distracters are diminishing people's capacity to listen, try to move the conversation to a more ideal location, such as a quieter room. Maybe try to limit the distractions by facing away from the extraneous stimuli. Further, team members should frequently check to make sure that they are understanding what is being said.

Table 6.7.   Tips for Improving Listening Skills

- Identify recurring or main themes.
- Note key words that are frequently used.
- Classify information in relevant categories.
- Take notes, but only write down important concepts.
- In your head, repeat important information.
- Visualize what the speaker is discussing.
- Ask clarifying questions, but only when needed.

Rehearsing responses.   Sometimes, when people get mad or emotional during a discussion, they will begin planning their rebuttal as the speaker is talking. As the listener is thinking about her response, she is likely to be missing what the speaker is saying. This is pretty common, especially in larger teams when not everybody can speak right away. So what can they do? One strategy is to take notes. As the thoughts regarding their response come to them, team members can jot down a couple key words that will remind them what they wanted to say. That way they don't have to rehearse things in order to remember them. Also, before responding to somebody, teammates should get into the habit of pausing for a few seconds to reflect on what they are about to say. This will help prevent them from saying something they'll regret later.

Daydreaming.   Another hindrance to good listening skills is daydreaming. Clearly, minds tend to wander when people are bored. However, some people's minds wander as soon as a conversation begins, especially if they have already had a long day. So, how can daydreamers focus their attention on what the speaker is saying?

One way is to become an active listener; that is, get involved in what is said. For example, team members can try to picture what the speaker is discussing. If the speaker is discussing how a student is behaving in her class, they can try to imagine the student's actions. Team members can also follow the speaker's main points by picturing an outline of the conversation in their head. Further, team members can try to anticipate what is going to be said next; however, they should not become so consumed with what might be said that they forget to hear what actually is being said.

Preconceived notions.   Many listeners will tune out speakers before the first word is uttered. This might be because the listener has preconceived notions about what the speaker is going to say. For example, perhaps the listener believes that he already knows everything about the speaker's topic and, as a result, feels that there is no reason to pay attention. Or maybe the listener is so confident that he won't like what is going to be said that he simply refuses to pay attention. Either way, preconceived notions can diminish a person's capacity to be a good listener. So what do you do? If team members believe that they know what is going to be discussed, they can actively compare their assumptions to what is actually said. If they believe that they already understand the topic at hand, listen to the speaker and attempt to find new information.

Or they can listen and identify information that supports or contradicts their understanding of the topic.

Understanding Non-Verbal Communication

Much of what people convey to others involves non-verbal communication. For example, suppose somebody says, "I am fine." Are they really fine? What if their teeth or hands are clenched? What message would he or she really be conveying? Needless to say, understanding non-verbal communication is paramount for team members to be effective. Here are three areas of non-verbal communication upon which people can focus.

Personal space.   There is a spatial nature of non-verbal communication. For example, how do you react when a speaker is standing very near to you? You are likely to look uncomfortable or back away. You might even feel threatened. What if the speaker stands too far away? You might believe that the speaker is aloof or doesn't care about you.

Difficulties with spatial issues are often confounded when people from different cultures interact. For example, many cultures in the United States prefer to have social interactions with people who are roughly an arm's length away. Some European cultures, however, tend to be much closer to people when they talk. These differences could create communication problems.

Body language.   Body language is an essential part of communication. Words alone only convey part of the speaker's message. For example, suppose that you ask a teacher if your child is behaving himself in class. The teacher says, "Oh, he is behaving himself alright." But she is also rolling her eyes and shaking her head. Does the teacher's verbal communication (i.e., what he says) match his non-verbal communication (i.e., what he did)?

Being aware of body language will really help team members understand what they are really trying to say. Further, being aware of your own body language will help convey the message you want to send. However, as with personal space, cultural differences could influence how people interpret non-verbal behavior. When in doubt, team members can simply ask for clarification. For example, they can say, "You say that my son is behaving himself, but I get the impression that he really isn't. Am I correct?"

Paralanguage.   In addition to how and where people stand, the way team members express messages will often dictate how people will interpret them. This is called paralanguage, the vocal part of language. This is not to be confused with the verbal part of language, which involves the words people choose. Paralanguage includes voice tone, pitch, volume, rhythm, and even the use of silence. Sarcasm is an excellent example. When sarcasm is used, it is the inflections and other vocal nuances that convey the desired message, not the actual words spoken.

Another example of paralanguage is the use of encouragers. Encouragers let speakers know that the listeners are listening. They include saying "Hmmmm", "Uh huh", and "Go on." Using these verbal cues can be overdone. For example, many times people will say "aha" when they are not really listening.

As with other non-verbal communication, team members should pay attention to how they say things just as much what you say. In noisy meeting rooms, speakers my feel tempted to increase the volume of their voice in order to be heard. However, speaking louder might lead others to believe that you are angry or frustrated. Instead of increasing their volume, speakers can move closer to the person to whom they are trying to communicate, wait until the buzz has died down in the room before they speak, or verbally acknowledge that they are raising their voice to be heard over the din.

Saying what is meant. Effective team members say what they mean. Words have subtle differences and can be taken several different ways. For example, suppose that somebody keeps asking questions that appear to be pointless. You could say "You are really frustrating me." Or you could say "I am becoming frustrated by all these questions."

The first statement implies that the person is trying to frustrate you on purpose. In response, the person might become defensive and their team role might become counterproductive. The second statement focuses upon the behavior (i.e., "the frequent questions") and not the team member. Further, the second statement does not indicate intent, which really isn't important at this point of the conversation.

STRATEGIES FOR ADDRESSING TROUBLE

No matter how effective each team member is, teams are bound to face some adversity. This is just natural. Teams are like people. They experience periods of change and growth. During these periods, conflict is likely. After all, conflict is a stimulus for change. How team members deal with these periods of conflict will often dictate how successful their team will become. Below are several problems that teams typically experience and potential solutions that might maximize the team's growth.

The Team Just Isn't Coming Together

Let suppose that you are really concerned about your child's behavior. Perhaps it is getting worse at both home or school. So you call a meeting with all of your child's teachers and special educators in order to generate some new ideas on how to handle the situation. When everybody gets together, the group of people never seems to coalesce into an effective team. In other words, they don't interact and they don't seem to view themselves as partners. How can these individuals build a team and get past the initial Forming Stage? Here are several suggestions.

- Have people describe themselves on an index card (what they like and dislike, where they grew up, trivia about themselves, etc.) shuffle the cards, and hand them out. Have the team members mingle, asking each other questions in an attempt to find the person on their card.
- Go around the table and have people introduce themselves— including what they do, why they agreed to be on the team, and a superlative fact about themselves (e.g., they once worked in the White House).
- Have team members pair up and interview each other. Then have the interviewers share what they learned with the rest of the group.
- Give each member a different "bingo card" with various experiences in each box (e.g., has sung in front of people, has been to Asia, is just like his or her mother, etc.). Call out the experiences. If somebody has had that experience, they tell the rest of the team about it. The team member who fills his or her card, completes three in a row, or doesn't have any of the announced experiences wins a silly prize.
- As a group, try to identify ten things that everybody in the team has in common.

Power Struggles

Once a team forms, there may be a period where team members define their roles. This period is likely to be very volatile, as discussed earlier. Several of the problems that you will face will likely involve power struggles. For example, members might dominate the conversation or vie for power. Maybe one or two team members think that they are completely right and everybody else is wrong. How can teams address power struggles? Here are a few suggestions.

- As a team, talk about expectations, including what they want to get from being a group member and how members should act. Doing this during the formation stage could help prevent problems before they start.
- Stick to the meeting's agreed upon rules and procedures. Do not change midstream unless the group as a whole feels it is appropriate.
- Agree to disagree. Realize that everybody might have a different perspective.
- Focus on the task at hand and not the conflict (see Table 6.8 for tips on dealing with conflict).
- Set time limits for each member to talk on each point.
- Remind people of the constructive feedback tips listed in Table 6.11.
- Offer to mediate the disagreement during break or after the meeting.
- Break the team into smaller work groups, making sure conflicting members are away from each other.

Trouble Getting Started

Let's suppose that a team formed, weathered the storm of Stage Two, but is having trouble getting down to business. Everybody understands

Table 6.8.   Ways of Dealing with Conflict within a Team

Strategy	Description
Agreeing to Disagree	Reducing the conflict by acknowledging there is a problem, but it will most likely never be solved.
Avoiding the Conflict	Refuse to get involved in the hopes that it will go away.
Compromising	Attempt to find a solution that is mutually palatable to the conflicting sides.
Pushing the Conflict	Forcing the conflicting sides to accept an outcome whether they like it or not.
Solving the Problem	Try to remove the cause of the conflict.

Table 6.9. Tips on Brainstorming

- Make sure everybody understands that the team is trying to generate as many ideas as possible.
- Refrain from commenting on, or critiquing, ideas as they are presented.
- Try to have people say whatever comes to mind.
- Don't "over think."
- Have a Recorder write down ideas on a board or someplace where everybody can see.
- Encourage people to list as many ideas as they can in a short period of time.
- Use previous ideas to generate new ideas.
- Use small groups (e.g., dyads) if people are reluctant to participate.
- When the number of ideas generated begin to wane, take a brief break or do an activity. Then come back to brainstorming a little later.

the goal of the group, but nobody can seem to find a good starting place. What can they do? Here are some ideas.

- Brainstorm possible options (see Table 6.9).
- Have each member break the team's overall goal into smaller, more manageable parts. Then describe the type of people who would be needed to accomplish each part. Have everybody report to the team as a whole.
- As a team, discuss how the team should be run, reasonable objectives for each meeting, best times to meet (morning, over lunch, etc.). Try to come to a consensus.
- Try to identify what is blocking the team's progress. Is the goal unimportant to the team members? Are there outside distracters (e.g. noise in the hallway)? Is everybody tired from a long day at work? Does the team lack the needed resources to complete the task? Once the potential cause is identified, eliminate it.
- Have a chart showing the team's progress.
- Assign tasks to team members and allow them to do them at home. They can then come back to the team and report what they have done.

Getting Back on Track

Once the team gets started, it will occasionally stall. For example, everybody is working fine but then little new progress is made. Perhaps, team members are starting to daydream or maybe they can't decide in which direction the team needs to go. Maybe they are going off on tangents. Perhaps everybody is getting tired. Either way, how can you help the team be productive again? Below are some suggestions.

- Backtrack to before everybody drifted away. Review the team's mission, what has been done, and what the task at hand is.
- Conduct an active activity. Perhaps have them get up and role-play.
- Take a short break.
- Have everybody get up and stretch.
- Move on to new business and table the topic causing the floundering.
- Refer frequently to the agenda.
- Bring attention to the fact that the team is getting off-track.
- Remove distractions.
- Redirect off-topic conversations back to the topic at hand.
- If all else fails, reschedule the meeting.

Some People Are Not Participating

The team is well on its way to accomplishing its goals, however some members do not participate in discussions. They just nod their heads or they go a long with what is said. Further, when the team breaks into work groups, the same members do very little. This is often the situation with regular educators who do not understand what is happening. Table 6.10 lists ideas on how to facilitate an effective discussion and get everybody involved.

- Make a point of asking opinion-related questions.
- Allow all to participate in ways other than talking in front of everybody (e.g., gathering information, writing the report, etc.)
- Ask nonpartcipants to lead an activity (e.g., brainstorming)
- Break the team in to dyads. It is hard to not participate when there is only one other person in the group.

Table 6.10.   How to Facilitate an Effective Discussion

- Make sure everybody understands the scope of the topic and the purpose of the discussion.
- Ask for clarification if people appear confused.
- Summarize key points.
- Synthesize divergent comments.
- Listen more than you speak.
- Bring people back on-task if they begin to digress or go on tangents.
- Keep the conversation moving. Don't let is dwell on any one point.
- Have the team set aside topics that are getting the conversation off-track.
- Periodically see if there is an agreement on what has been said.
- Manage the team's time so that the discussion can reach its natural conclusion.

Table 6.11.   Tips on Giving Constructive Feedback

- Provide positive feedback regularly.
- Do not ever consider feedback "negative." Consider it "things to work on" or "future positives."
- Positives comments should out number critic comments.
- Be descriptive of what is good and what needs work.
- Be precise.
- Don't exaggerate accomplishments or shortcomings.
- Speak only of the issue, not perceived motivation or the person's character.
- Don't be overwhelming. Be brief.
- Allow time to digest information.
- Allow for feedback.
- Pay attention to nonverbal language (yours and the listener's).
- End on a positive note.

- Make sure people feel welcome to participate. Create accepting environments.

Some People Just Want to Get Done

On occasion, some of team members will just want to finish the meeting or complete the IEP without regard to quality. These individuals might simply agree with the majority without giving much thought to what is at stake. Or they might push through ideas without allowing the team to consider other options. Here are some suggestions on how to encourage members to slow down and produce quality work.

- Hold secret votes.
- Always generate multiple options before deciding on the course of action.
- Have the team list strengths and weaknesses of each idea.
- Remind the team of the importance of the team's mission at the beginning of each meeting.
- Make sure everybody is satisfied before the team moves on to the next topic.

APPLYING WHAT YOU HAVE LEARNED

Go back to the beginning of the chapter and read the case study regarding the Ussak's IEP meeting. Apply what you have learned in this chapter to their situation. What have you learned?

Question #1: Why Didn't The Ussaks Participant?

Why didn't the Ussaks participate in the meeting? There are literally dozens of potential reasons. But which is most likely the real cause? Without understanding the reason, or reasons, for their lack of participation, it will be difficult to encourage them to be more active team members—as discussed later. Some potential reasons for their behavior may include:

- The hostile environment (created mainly by Mr. Pelleck) made them feel defensive and, as a method of coping with their situation, the Ussaks simply chose not to participate.
- The Ussaks did not realize that they were involved with the team. Perhaps they believed questions directed at them were simply out of courtesy and that there was no point in responding since everybody else made the final decisions.
- Their lack of participation could be culturally based. The surname "Ussak" is Inuit. Many Inuit cultures hold teachers in very high esteem, and it is customary to listen to teachers, not to speak to teachers or tell them what you think. This would explain why both parents and Sally do not actively engage teachers in conversation. It should be noted that Inuits often will blink in the same manner as many people nod their heads. So if they wish to send a non-verbal message to a speaker, they will blink their eyes—a communication style that is likely to be misinterpreted by non-Inuits. So, perhaps, the Ussaks were participating and the rest of the IEP team didn't know it.

**Question #2: How Can Mrs. Denver Increase
The Ussak's Participation?**

So, how could Mrs. Denver encourage the Ussaks to participate? As alluded to above, the strategies that teachers might select will depend largely upon why the Ussaks are not participating in the first place. For example, if the hostile environment is inhibiting their participation, Mrs. Denver's strategy will need to create a more supportive, and accepting, milieu. Perhaps the IEP team could meet in a neutral environment, such as a coffee shop or restaurant. Or team members can eliminate the hostility that is coming from some of the team members (e.g., Mr. Pelleck), as will be discussed shortly.

On the other hand, if culture is causing the lack of participation, Mrs. Denver might wish to learn more about the Ussak's beliefs. Perhaps, she could have them teach other team member about themselves and their culture. This could help build a greater sense of belonging to the team, thus encouraging more participation.

Question #3: What Roles Did Mr. Pelleck Play?

What roles did Mr. Pelleck play in the IEP meeting? Certainly, he is a "Dominator." He took control of the meeting and didn't let anybody get a word in edgewise. Further, when others started to speak, he would interrupt and redirect the focus of the meeting on him.

Mr. Pelleck may also be considered a "Blocker." Whenever teammates tried to voice an opinion that might be different from his, he would tell them that they were wrong. He did this to Miss McAfee when she started to say something positive about Sally remaining in Regular Education classes. Further, he prevented Mr. Horwitz from even speaking.

He might also be an "Opinion Giver." Notice how nobody asked him what he thought about students with special needs. Yet, everybody probably knew exactly how he felt about the subject!

As Mr. Pelleck illustrates, people can assume many different roles at the same time. Often, these roles are not very productive. By understanding what roles people play, more effective teams can be developed, as will be discussed next.

Question #4: How Can Teams Become More Effective?

Mrs. Denver not only has to coordinate an IEP team and attempt to accomplish its goal (i.e., determining Sally's Least Restrictive Environment), but she also has to defuse a very hostile situation, as well as get Sally's parents more involved. How could she make the I.E.P. team more effective?

As discussed earlier, Mrs. Denver needs to get everybody involved in the discussion. This would entail not only understanding the Ussaks' culture and expectations, but also minimizing Mr. Pelleck's negative effects on the team. She should also try to utilize the knowledge and skills of the rest of her team members.

To understand the Ussaks' culture, Mrs. Denver can simply ask the Ussaks questions. Or she could access other resources available to her.

For example, go on the Internet and "chat" with other people who are Inuit. Check out books from the library. Maybe make a home visit and observe the family unit. Without understanding her team members, it is difficult to develop an effective team.

Mrs. Denver could also get together with the Ussaks apart from the team before and after the meeting. This may help them feel less overwhelmed and more prepared to participate. Specifically, talking outside the meeting might give them an opportunity to ask questions that they normally would be too embarrassed to ask in front of everybody else. Further, meeting away from the team could give the Ussaks additional time to process what has been said.

To minimize Mr. Pelleck's domination of the proceedings, Mrs. Denver might want to consider a formal agenda. Allow everybody to present their information and then have people make comments afterwards. This would enable everybody to say something without being interrupted by Mr. Pelleck. If Mr. Pelleck continues to prevent people from presenting their viewpoints, Mrs. Denver could politely remind him of the agenda and to save what he wants to say until his turn.

Mrs. Denver could also institute a five-minute rule which would limit the amount of discussion on any one topic to five minutes, or whatever time frame she desired. Such a rule would help prevent any one member from dominating the conversation. This is a particularly effective strategy for preventing meetings from dragging on and on. However, don't forget that sometimes teams will need to really discuss a topic in depth. For these occasions, Mrs. Denver could waive the time restrictions and allow people as much time as they need.

To utilize everybody's knowledge and skills, Mrs. Denver could break people into smaller groups and have them complete certain activities. For example, perhaps have the small groups brainstorm ways of helping Sally succeed in regular education. Or have each team member share strategies that they use to help Sally in their classroom.

CHAPTER 7

Resources for Families, Professionals, and Individuals with Disabilities

INTRODUCTION

Within this chapter are resources that parents, teachers, and family members of children with disabilities might find useful. Specifically, various organizations, books, and websites are discussed below. Inclusion within this chapter does not mean that these resources are endorsed or supported in any way. Further, some of the information presented may have changed since this book's publication. Please go directly to the source for updated information.

ORGANIZATIONS AND WEB SITES

The organizations and web sites presented in this section are categorized by condition. However, please note that many organizations are excellent resources for multiple disabilities. Further, most web sites have links to other sources of information. You may want to keep a running list of resources that are useful for you. Perhaps write them in the margin of this book so that you can find them again when they are needed.

Mental Retardation and Related Conditions

Organization: Best Buddies

Mission Statement: Best Buddies establishes one-to-one friendships between people with mental retardation and college students, high school students, middle school students and members of the community.

Mailing Address:

100 SE Second Street, #1990

Miami, FL 33131

E-Mail Address: LaverneL@BestBuddies.org
Phone Number: (305) 374-2233

Organization: American Association on Mental Retardation
Mission Statement: AAMR promotes progressive policies, sound
   research, effective practices, and universal human rights for people
   with intellectual disabilities.
Mailing Address:
   444 North Capitol Street, NW Suite 846
   Washington, D.C. 20001-1512
E-Mail Address: www.aamr.org
Phone Number: (800) 424-3688

Organization: The Arc of the United States
Mission Statement: The Arc is the national organization of and for
   people with mental retardation and related developmental disabilities and their families. It is devoted to promoting and improving
   supports and services for people with mental retardation and their
   families. The association also fosters research and education regarding the prevention of mental retardation in infants and young
   children.
Mailing Address:
   1010 Wayne Ave., Suite 650
   Silver Spring, MD 20910
E-Mail Address: Info@thearc.org
Phone Number: (301) 565-3842

Organization: TASH (The Association for Persons with Severe Handicaps)
Mission Statement: TASH is an international association of people
   with disabilities, their family members, other advocates, and professionals fighting for a society in which inclusion of all people in
   all aspects of society is the norm.
Mailing Address:
   29. W. Susquehanna Ave., Suite 210
   Baltimore, MD 21204
E-Mail Address: http://tash.org/
Phone Number: 1-800-482-8274

Organization: National Association for Down Syndrome

Mission Statement: To promote an environment which fosters the growth and development of people with Down syndrome to enable them to achieve their full potential, to provide support and information on Down syndrome to parents, and to disseminate up-to-date information on Down syndrome

Mailing Address:
P.O. Box 4542
Oak Brook, IL 60522
E-Mail Address: http://www.nads.org
Phone Number: (630) 325-9112

Organization: National Down Syndrome Society

Mission Statement: The National Down Syndrome Society was established in 1979 to ensure that all people with Down syndrome have the opportunity to achieve their full potential in community life.

Mailing Address:
666 Broadway
New York, NY 10012
E-Mail Address: www.ndss.org
Phone Number: (800) 221-4602

Organization: Brain Injury Association

Mission Statement: The mission of Brain Injury Association is to create a better future through brain injury prevention, research, education, and advocacy.

Mailing Address:
105 North Alfred Street
Alexandria, VA 22314
E-Mail/Web Address: www.biausa.org
Phone Number: (703) 236-6000

Organization: The Perspective's Network- Survive With Pride!

Mission Statement: The Perspectives Network, Inc.'s primary focus is positive communication between persons with brain injury, family members/ caregivers/friends of persons with brain injury, those many professionals who treat persons with brain injury and community members in order to create positive changes and enhance public awareness and knowledge of acquired/traumatic brain injury.

Mailing Address:

P.O. Box 1859

Cumming, GA 30028-1859

E-Mail/Web Address: TPN@tib.org

Phone Number:

Autism, Asperger's, and Pervasive Developmental Disorders

Organization: Autism Society of America

Mission Statement: The mission of the Autism Society of America is to promote lifelong access and opportunity for all individuals within the autism spectrum, and their families, to be fully participating, included members of their community. Education, advocacy at state and federal levels, active public awareness and the promotion of research form the cornerstones of ASA's efforts to carry forth its mission.

Mailing Address:

7910 Woodmont Avenue, Suite 300

Bethesda, Maryland 20814-3067

E-Mail/Web Address: asaf@autism-society.org

Phone Number: (800) 3AU-TISM

Organization: Autism Network International

Mission Statement: Autism Network International is an autistic-run self-help and advocacy organization for autistic people.

Mailing Address:

P.O. Box 35448

Syracuse NY 13235-5448

E-Mail/Web Address: www.ani.autistics.org/

Organization: National Alliance for Autism Research

Mission Statement: The National Alliance for Autism Research, NAAR, is a national nonprofit, tax-exempt organization dedicated to finding the causes, prevention, effective treatment and, ultimately, cure of the autism spectrum disorders.

Mailing Address:

99 Wall St., Research Park

Princeton, New Jersey 08540

E-Mail/Web Address: naar@naar.org
Phone Number: (888) 777-NAAR

Learning Disabilities

Organization: Council for Exceptional Children
Mission Statement: CEC, a non-profit association, accomplishes its mission which is carried out in support of special education professionals and others working on behalf of individuals with exceptionalities, by advocating for appropriate governmental policies, by setting professional standards, by providing continuing professional development, by advocating for newly and historically underserved individuals with exceptionalities, and by helping professionals achieve the conditions and resources necessary for effective professional practice.
Mailing Address:
1920 Association Drive
Reston, VA 22091-1589
E-Mail/Web Address: www.cec.sped.org/
Phone Number: (703) 620-3660

Organization: Learning Disabilities Association of America
Mission Statement: Non-profit organization dedicated to identifying causes and promoting prevention of learning disabilities and to enhance the quality of life for all individuals with learning disabilities and their families by encouraging effective identification and intervention, fostering research, and protecting their rights under law. LDA seeks to accomplish this through awareness, advocacy, empowerment, education, service and collaborative efforts.
Mailing Address:
4156 Library Road
Pittsburgh, PA 15234-1349
E-Mail/Web Address: info@ldaamerica.org
Phone Number: (412) 341-1515

Organization: International Dyslexia Association
Mission Statement: The International Dyslexia Association (IDA) is a non-profit organization dedicated to helping individuals with dyslexia, their families and the communities that support them. IDA is the oldest learning disabilities organization in the nation—founded in 1949 in memory of Dr. Samuel T. Orton, a distinguished

neurologist. Throughout our rich history, our goal has been to provide the most comprehensive forum for parents, educators, and researchers to share their experiences, methods, and knowledge.

Mailing Address:

Chester Building, Suite 382

8600 LaSalle Road

Baltimore, MD 21286-2044

E-Mail/Web Address: info@interdys.org

Phone Number: (800) 222-3123

Organization: National Association for the Education of African American Children with Learning Disabilities

Mission Statement: The National Association for the Education of African American Children with Learning Disabilities (NAEAA-CLD) was founded in 1999 for the purpose of increasing awareness and promoting an understanding of the specific issues facing African American children. The organization's mission is to link information and resources provided by an established network of individuals and organizations experienced in minority research and special education with parents, educators, and others responsible for providing a quality education for all students.

Mailing Address:

P.O. Box 09521

Columbus, Ohio 43209

E-Mail/Web Address: info@aacld.org

Phone Number: (614) 237-6021

Organization: National Center for Learning Disabilities

Mission Statement: The mission of the National Center for Learning Disabilities (NCLD) is to increase opportunities for all individuals with learning disabilities to achieve their potential. NCLD accomplishes its mission by increasing public awareness and understanding of learning disabilities, conducting educational programs and services that promote research-based knowledge, and providing national leadership in shaping public policy. We provide solutions that help people with LD participate fully in society.

Mailing Address:

381 Park Avenue South, Suite 1420

New York, NY 10016

E-Mail/Web Address:
Phone Number: (888) 575-7373

Organization: National Coalition on Auditory Processing Disorders
Mission Statement: The mission of the National Coalition on Auditory Processing Disorders, Inc. is to assist families and individuals affected by auditory processing disorders through education, support, and public awareness as well as promoting auditory access of information for those affected by auditory processing disorders.
Mailing Address:
P.O. Box 11810
Jacksonville, Fl 32239-1810
E-Mail/Web Address: info@ncapd.org
Phone Number: (904)-743-4300

Behavior Disorders

Organization: ANAD Anorexia Nervosa and Associated Disorders
Mission Statement: To prevent eating disorders. Prevention programs are continuous and are carried through in a professional manner. Packets are sent to primary and secondary schools, colleges and universities, groups and associations.
Mailing Address:
Po Box 7
Highland Park, IL 60035
E-Mail/Web Address: info@anad.org
Phone Number: (847) 831-3438

Organization: Family Resources for Education on Eating Disorders (FREED)
Mission Statement: A parent-founded, non-profit, organization committed to educating our community about the serious nature and growing prevalence of anorexia, bulimia, and binge eating disorder; providing information about how to recognize and treat eating disorders; and providing resources for support for persons suffering from an eating disorder and for their families and friends.
Mailing Address:
9611 Page Avenue
Bethesda, MD 20814-1737

E-Mail/Web Address: www.cpcug.org/user/rpike/freed.html
Phone Number: (301) 585-0358

Organization: The National Depressive and Manic-Depressive Association
Mission Statement: To educate patients families, professionals and the public concerning the nature of depressive and manic-depressive illness as treatable medical diseases; to foster self-help for patients and families; to eliminate discrimination and stigma; to improve access to care; and to advocate for research toward the elimination of these illnesses.
Mailing Address:
730 N. Franklin Street, Suite 501,
Chicago, Illinois 60610-7204
E-Mail/Web Address: www.ndmda.org/findsupport.html
Phone Number: (800) 826-3632

Organization: National Alliance for the Mentally Ill
Mission Statement: The National Alliance for the Mentally Ill (NAMI) is a nonprofit, grassroots, self-help, support and advocacy organization of consumers, families, and friends of people with severe mental illnesses, such as schizophrenia, major depression, bipolar disorder, obsessive-compulsive disorder, and anxiety disorders.
Mailing Address:
Colonial Place Three, 2107 Wilson Blvd., Suite 300,
Arlington, VA 22201
E-Mail/Web Address: www.NAMI.org
Phone Number: 1-800-950-NAMI [6264]

Organization: Anxiety Disorder Association of America
Mission Statement: The Anxiety Disorders Association of America (ADAA) is a nonprofit organization whose mission is to promote the prevention, treatment and cure of anxiety disorders and to improve the lives of all people who suffer from them. Since 1980, by disseminating information, linking people who need treatment with those who can provide it and advocating for cost effective treatments, the ADAA has made it possible for hundreds of thousands of individuals to benefit from its services and publications. The association is made up of professionals who conduct research

and treat anxiety disorders and individuals who have a personal or general interest in learning more about such disorders.

Mailing Address:

11900 Parklawn Drive, Suite 100

Rockville, MD 20852, USA

E-Mail/Web Address: anxdis@adaa.org

Phone Number: (301) 231-9350

Organization: Council for Children with Behavioral Disorders

Mission Statement: The Council for Children with Behavioral Disorders (CCBD) is the official division of the Council for Exceptional Children (CEC) committed to promoting and facilitating the education and general welfare of children and youth with emotional or behavioral disorders.

Mailing Address:

1920 Association Drive

Reston, Virginia 20191-1589

E-Mail/Web Address: http://www.ccbd.net/index.cfm

Phone Number:

Organization: The Federation of Families for Children's Mental Health

Mission Statement: The Federation of Families for Children's Mental Health services, with humility and determination, to provide and sustain leadership for a broad and deep nationwide network of family-run organizations. We harness the passion (and we honor the cultural diversity) of our national membership and focus it as a potent force for change in behalf of children with mental needs and their families. We are passionate advocates at the national level for the rights of these children and families. We are equally passionate in transferring our insights and experiences to statewide family organizations, local chapter, and other family-run organizations so that skillful and effective advocacy can occur at state and local levels as well. We extend a lifeline to this network so that our partner organizations might draw strength from us and, in turn, better respond to the needs of families requiring guidance, training, support, and personal advocacy. Through our new visions that enrich the capacities of our partner, strengthen our network, and allow us to serve with pride in this leadership role.

Mailing Address:
1101 King Street, Suite 420
Alexandria, VA 22314
E-Mail/Web Address: www.ffcmh.org
Phone Number: (703) 684-7710

Organization: NSF (National Schizophrenia Foundation)
Mission Statement: It is the mission of the National Schizophrenia Foundation (NSF) to pursue the development and maintenance of support groups for individuals, and their friends and family members, affected by schizophrenia and related disorders, and to be a broad resource for all persons regarding schizophrenia and related disorders through education, information, and public awareness services.
Mailing Address:
403 Seymour Street, Suite 202
Lansing, MI 48933
E-Mail/Web Address: www.sanonymous.org/
Phone Number: (800) 482-9534

Attention Deficit Hyperactivity Disorders

Organization: Children and Adults with Attention Deficit Hyperactivity Disorder
Mission Statement: CHADD works to improve the lives of people affected by AD/HD through Collaborative Leadership, Advocacy, Research, Education, and Support.
Mailing Address:
499 NW 70th Avenue, Suite 109
Plantation, FL 33317
E-Mail/Web Address: www.chadd.org
Phone Number: (800) 233-4050

Organization: ADD Group
Mission Statement: The ADD Action Group is a non-profit organization that helps people find alternative solutions for ADD, learning differences, dyslexia, and autism.
Mailing Address:
ADD Action Group
PO Box 1440

Ansonia Station
New York NY 10023
E-Mail/Web Address:
Phone Number: (212) 769-2457

Organization: Attention Deficit Disorder Association
Mission Statement: ADDA's mission is to help people with ADD lead happier, more successful lives through education, research, and public advocacy. Whether you have ADD yourself, or someone special in your life does, or you treat, counsel, or teach those who do, ADDA is an organization for you.
Mailing Address:
1788 Second Street, Suite 200
Highland Park, IL 60035
E-Mail/Web Address: mail@add.org
Phone Number: (847) 432-ADDA

Physical Disabilities

Organization: The National Spinal Cord Injury Association
Mission Statement: The mission of The National Spinal Cord Injury Association (NSCIA) is to educate, and empower survivors of spinal cord injury and disease through our toll-free help-line, nationwide chapters and support groups to achieve and maintain higher levels of independence.
Mailing Address:
545 Concord Avenue, Suite 29
Cambridge, MA 02138
E-Mail/Web Address: www.spinalcord.org
Phone Number: (800) 962-9629

Organization: American Paraplegia Society.
Mission Statement: APS is organized and functions exclusively for scientific and educational purposes. Its goals are to advance SCI patient care, promote research and education related to spinal cord impairment, provide a forum for the review of scientific findings and recognize physicians and researchers whose careers are devoted to the problems of spinal cord impairment.

Mailing Address:
7520 Astoria Blvd.
Jackson Heights, NY 11370
E-Mail/Web Address: www.apssci.org
Phone Number: (718) 803-3782

Organization: Spinal Cord Society

Mission Statement: SCS is a large grass roots organization linked by over 200 chapters, a monthly Newsletter, and thousands of members throughout North America and 24 other countries. Its goal is cure of spinal cord injury paralysis. It is an organization of the spinal cord injured, their families and friends, and dedicated scientists and physicians who are aiming at the ultimate goal of cure through improved treatment and research.

Mailing Address:
19051 County Highway 1
Fergus Falls, Minnesota 56537-7609
E-Mail/Web Address: http://members.aol.com/scsweb/private/ scshome.htm
Phone Number: (218) 739-5252

Organization: Muscular Dystrophy Association

Mission Statement: A dedicated partnership between scientists and concerned citizens aimed at conquering neuromuscular diseases that affect more than a million Americans.

Mailing Address:
National Headquarters
3300 E. Sunrise Dr.
Tucson, AZ 85718
E-Mail/Web Address: www.mdausa.org
Phone Number: (800) 572-1717

Organization: Parent Project Muscular Dystrophy

Mission Statement: The Parent Project Muscular Dystrophy mobilizes people in the United States and Worldwide in collaborative effort to enable people with Duchenne and Becker Muscular Dystrophy to survive, thrive and fully participate within their families and communities into adulthood and beyond.

Mailing Address:
  1012 North University Blvd
  Middletown, OH 45042
E-Mail/Web Address: www.parentdmd.org
Phone Number: (800) 714-KIDS

Organization: Epilepsy Foundation
Mission Statement: The Epilepsy Foundation is a national, charitable
  organization, founded in 1968 as the Epilepsy Foundation of
  America. The only such organization wholly dedicated to the wel-
  fare of people with epilepsy, our mission is simple: to work for
  children and adults affected by seizures through research, educa-
  tion, advocacy and service.
Mailing Address:
  4351 Garden City Drive
  Landover, MD 20785-7223
E-Mail/Web Address: www.efa.org
Phone Number: (800) 332-1000

Organization: MS Central Awareness
Mission Statement: To provide information and service to achieve a
  more rewarding and buoyant life experience for those with MS, a long
  term, nonfatal neurological disease with no known cure. Our goal is to
  provide self-awareness and educate the public at large about the health
  and lifestyle challenges facing those affected with the disease.
Mailing Address:
  P.O. Box 1193
  Venice, Fl 34284
E-Mail/Web Address: www.msawareness.org
Phone Number: (888) 336-MSAF

Sensory and Communication Impairments

Organization: National Institute on Deafness and Other Communication Disorders
Mission Statement: The National Institute on Deafness and Other
  Communication Disorders (NIDCD) is one of the Institutes that
  comprise the National Institutes of Health (NIH). NIH is the Federal
  government's focal point for the support of biomedical research.

NIH's mission is to uncover new knowledge that will lead to better health for everyone. Simply described, the goal of NIH research is to acquire new knowledge to help prevent, detect, diagnose, and treat disease and disability. NIH is part of the U.S. Department of Health and Human Services.

Mailing Address:

31 Center Drive, MSC 2320

Bethesda, MD USA 20892-2320

E-Mail/Web Address: http://www.nidcd.nih.gov/

Phone Number: (301) 496-7243

Organization: American Speech-Language-Hearing Association (ASHA)

Mission Statement: The American Speech-Language-Hearing Association (ASHA) is the professional, scientific, and credentialing association for more than 103,000 audiologists, speech-language pathologists, and speech, language, and hearing scientists. ASHA's mission is to ensure that all people with speech, language, and hearing disorders have access to quality services to help them communicate more effectively.

Mailing Address:

10801 Rockville Pike

Rockville, MD 20852

E-Mail/Web Address: http://www.asha.org/

Phone Number: (800) 638-8255

Organization: Center for Speech and Language Disorders

Mission Statement: We are a non-profit organization based in Elmhurst, Illinois. Our mission is to help children with speech and language disorders reach their full potential.

Mailing Address:

195 W Spangler, Suite B

Elmhurst IL 60126

E-Mail/Web Address: http://www.csld.com/

Phone Number: (630) 530-8551

Organization: National Association of the Deaf

Mission Statement: The mission of the National Association of the Deaf is to promote, protect, and preserve the rights and quality of life of deaf and hard of hearing individuals in the United States of America.

Mailing Address: National Association of the Deaf
814 Thayer Avenue
Silver Spring, MD 20910-4500
E-Mail/Web Address: http://www.nad.org/
Phone Number: 301-587-1788

Organization: American Council for the Blind
Mission Statement: The Council strives to improve the well-being of all blind and visually impaired people by: serving as a representative national organization of blind people; elevating the social, economic and cultural levels of blind people; improving educational and rehabilitation facilities and opportunities; cooperating with the public and private institutions and organizations concerned with blind services; encouraging and assisting all blind persons to develop their abilities and conducting a public education program to promote greater understanding of blindness and the capabilities of blind people.
Mailing Address:
1155 15th Street, NW, Suite 1004,
Washington, DC 20005
E-Mail/Web Address: www.acb.org
Phone Number: (800) 424-8666

Organization: National Federation of the Blind
Mission Statement: The purpose of the National Federation of the Blind is twofold—to help blind persons achieve self-confidence and self-respect and to act as a vehicle for collective self-expression by the blind. By providing public education about blindness, information and referral services, scholarships, literature and publications about blindness, aids and appliances and other adaptive equipment for the blind, advocacy services and protection of civil rights, Job Opportunities for the Blind, development and evaluation of technology, and support for blind persons and their families, members of the NFB strive to educate the public that the blind are normal individuals who can compete on terms of equality.
Mailing Address:
1800 Johnson Street
Baltimore, MD 21230

E-Mail/Web Address: nfb@nfb.org
Phone Number: (410) 659-9314

Gifted and Talented

Organization: National Association for Gifted Children (NAGC)

Mission Statement: The National Association for Gifted Children
(NAGC) is an organization of parents, teachers, educators, other
professionals and community leaders who unite to address the
unique needs of children and youth with demonstrated gifts and
talents as well as those children who may be able to develop their
talent potential with appropriate educational experiences. We support and develop policies and practices that encourage and respond
to the diverse expressions of gifts and talents in children and youth
from all cultures, racial and ethnic backgrounds, and socioeco-
nomic groups. NAGC supports and engages in research and development, staff development, advocacy, communication, and collaboration with other organizations and agencies who strive to
improve the quality of education for all students.

Mailing Address:

1707 L Street, NW Suite 550

Washington, DC 20036

E-Mail/Web Address: www.nagc.org

Phone Number: (202) 785-4268

Organization: The National Foundation for Gifted and Creative Children

Mission Statement: The National Foundation for Gifted and Creative
Children was formed over 30 years ago. The main goal of The
Foundation was to get much needed information to the parents of
gifted children. The need is still there. Many gifted children are being destroyed in the public education system. Many gifted children
are being falsely labeled with ADD as well as ADHD. And many
parents are unaware their child/children could be potentially
gifted. The Foundation's main objective is to reach out and help
these precious children.

Mailing Address:

395 Diamond Hill Road

Warwick, Rhode Island 02886-8554

E-Mail/Web Address: www.nfgcc.org
Phone Number: (401) 738-0937

Organization: The Gifted Child Society
Mission Statement: The Gifted Child Society is a non-profit organization that was founded in 1957 by parents in New Jersey to further the
cause of gifted children. It's mission goals are: educational enrich-
ment and support services specifically designed for gifted children,
assistance to parents in raising gifted children to full and productive
adulthood, professional training to encourage educators to meet the
special needs of these youngsters, and a greater effort to win public
recognition and acceptance of these special need.
Mailing Address:
190 Rock Road,
Glen Rock, New Jersey 07452-1736
E-Mail/Web Address: admin@gifted.org
Phone Number: (201) 444-6530

Organization: Mensa
Mission Statement: As an organization, American Mensa provides
intelligent individuals an opportunity to meet other smart people at
the local, regional, and national levels. Mensans interact at enter-
taining events and exchange ideas through a variety of publications. Mensa members also work to help others in their communities
by providing scholarships and volunteering for community-oriented
activities.
Mailing Address:
1229 Corporate Drive West
Arlington, TX 76006-6103
E-Mail/Web Address: AmericanMensa@mensa.org
Phone Number: 1-800-66-MENSA

BOOKS

All of the following books, and the information about them, are from
www. Amazon.com. Inclusion of a resource does not imply support for
these texts. New editions are likely to be produced after the publication
of a cited text, so you may want to check with your local bookstore to
see if there are updated copies.

Mental Retardation and Related Conditions

Title: Steps to Independence: Teaching Everyday Skills to Children with Special Needs, Third Edition

Author(s): Bruce L. Baker, Alan J. Brightman, Jan B. Blacher, Louis J Heifetz, Stephen P. Hinshaw, Diane M. Murphy

Miscellaneous Information: Paperback—392 pages 3rd edition (January 1997) Paul H Brookes Pub Co; ISBN: 1557662681

Brief Description: Now in its third edition, this step-by-step guide to teaching everyday skills to children with special needs has been a popular resource for more than 20 years. Updated with even more practical teaching tips than in previous editions and an expanded section on behavior problem management, this friendly, parent-oriented book covers toilet training, play, self-help skills, information skills, advanced living skills, and more. In addition to helpful features such as sample activities, case examples, skills inventories, and cartoon illustrations, this easy-to-use sourcebook contains a new chapter devoted to computers that offers advice on using technology to enhance children's learning.

Title: Teaching Students with Mental Retardation: A Life Goal Curriculum Planning Approach

Author(s): Glen E. Thomas

Miscellaneous Information: Hardcover—597 pages 1 edition (February 5, 1996) Prentice Hall; ISBN: 0024202401

Brief Description: This book emphasizes and identifies (1) a prioritized life goal curriculum planning approach to identify the functional skills and concepts needed by a student with mental retardation or severe disabilities to become as successful as possible in adult life, and (2) a diagnostic/prescriptive teaching approach to assess each student's abilities and progress toward those individual life goals.

Title: The Mental Retardation and Developmental Disability Treatment Planner

Author(s): Arthur E. Jongsma Jr., Kellye Slaggert, Arthur E., Jr. Jongsma

Miscellaneous Information: Paperback—288 pages (July 2000) John Wiley & Sons; ISBN: 0471382531

Brief Description: Patterned after the best-selling The Complete Psychotherapy Treatment Planner, this sourcebook provides an array of pre-written treatment plan components for the mentally retarded and developmentally disabled.

Title: Down Syndrome: A Review of Current Knowledge
Author(s): J. A. Rondal (Editor), Juan Perera (Editor), Lynn Nadel (Editor)
Miscellaneous Information: Paperback—242 pages (May 1, 1999) Whurr Pub Ltd; ISBN: 1861560621
Brief Description: Papers presented at the Sixth World Congress on Down Syndrome held in Madrid, Spain, in October 1997. Focuses on scientific advances and therapeutic practices. Discusses independence, education, psychology, communication, medicine, genetics, and Down syndrome in the world.

Title: Handbook of Mental Retardation and Development
Author(s): Jacob A. Burack (Editor), Robert M. Hodapp (Editor), Edward Zigler (Editor)
Miscellaneous Information: Paperback—608 pages (March 1998) Cambridge Univ Press; ISBN: 0521446686
Brief Description: This book reviews theoretical and empirical work in the developmental approach to mental retardation. Armed with methods derived from the study of typically developing children, developmentalists have recently learned about the mentally retarded child's own development in a variety of areas. These areas now encompass many aspects of cognition, language, social and adaptive functioning, as well as of maladaptive behavior and psychopathology. This handbook provides a comprehensive guide to understanding mental retardation.

Title: Children With Mental Retardation : A Parents' Guide (The Special Needs Collection)
Author(s): Romayne Smith (Editor)
Miscellaneous Information: Paperback (May 1993) Woodbine House; ISBN: 0933149395
Brief Description: A book for parents of children with mental retardation, whether or not they have a diagnosed syndrome or condition. It provides a complete introduction to a child's medical,

therapeutic, and educational needs and covers topics such as family adjustment, daily care, child development, early intervention, special education, and legal rights. A reading list, a glossary of important terms, and a national listing of disability organizations make this a complete handbook.

Title: Mental Retardation: Nature, Cause, and Management
Author(s): George S. Baroff
Miscellaneous Information: Paperback—500 pages 3rd edition (June 1999) Taylor & Francis; ISBN: 1583910018
Brief Description: Provides recent material on the major dimensions of mental retardation: its nature, its causes, both biology and psychological, and its management.

Title: Differences in Common : Straight Talk on Mental Retardation, Down Syndrome, and Your Life
Author(s): Marilyn Trainer, Helen Featherstone
Miscellaneous Information: Paperback—236 pages (November 1991) Woodbine House; ISBN: 0933149409
Brief Description: A writer's collection of almost fifty essays that span more than 20 years of her experience as the mother of a son with Down syndrome. With poignancy and humor, Trainer explores a wide variety of issues, including family adjustment, public attitudes, inclusion, and independence. While her insights and nuggets of wisdom are shaped by the joys and frustration of raising a child with mental retardation, they often strike a common chord in all of us.

Title: Equal Treatment for People With Mental Retardation : Having and Raising Children
Author(s): Martha A. Field, Valerie A. Sanchez
Miscellaneous Information: Hardcover—448 pages (February 2000) Harvard Univ Pr; ISBN: 0674800869
Brief Description: Engaging in sex, becoming parents, raising children: these are among the most personal decisions we make, and for people with mental retardation, these decisions are consistently challenged, regulated, and outlawed. This book is a comprehensive study of the American legal doctrines and social policies, past and present, that have governed procreation and parenting by people with mental retardation.

Autism, Asperger's, and Pervasive Developmental Disorders

Title: Educating Children With Autism

Author(s): National Research Council

Miscellaneous Information: Hardcover—324 pages 1st edition (October 2001) National Academy Press; ISBN: 0309072697

Brief Description: Educating Children with Autism outlines an interdisciplinary approach to education for children with autism. The committee explores what makes education effective for the child with autism and identifies specific characteristics of programs that work. Recommendations are offered for choosing educational content and strategies, introducing interaction with other children, and other key areas.

Title: Thinking in Pictures : And Other Reports from My Life With Autism

Author(s): Temple Grandin

Miscellaneous Information: Paperback—222 pages 1 Vintage edition (November 1996) Vintage Books; ISBN: 0679772898

Brief Description: Temple Grandin, Ph.D., is a gifted animal scientist who has designed one third of all the livestock-handling facilities in the United States. She also lectures widely on autism because she is autistic, a woman who thinks, feels, and experiences the world in ways that are incomprehensible to the rest of us. In this unprecedented book, Grandin writes from the dual perspectives of a scientist and an autistic person. She tells us how she managed to breach the boundaries of autism to function in the outside world. What emerges is the document of an extraordinary human being, one who gracefully bridges the gulf between her condition and our own while shedding light on our common identity.

Title: Facing Autism : Giving Parents Reasons for Hope and Guidance for Help

Author(s): Lynn M. Hamilton, Bernard Rimland

Miscellaneous Information: Paperback—366 pages (March 14, 2000) Waterbrook Pr; ISBN: 1578562627

Brief Description: Now parents of autistic children can find the hope and practical guidance they need. Perhaps one of the most devastating things parents can learn is that their child has been diagnosed with autism. A multifaceted disorder, autism has long baffled parents and professionals alike. At one time, doctors gave parents virtually no hope for combating the disorder. But in recent years, new treatments and therapies have demonstrated that improvement is possible. With intensive, early intervention, some children have recovered from autism and have been integrated into school, indistinguishable from their peers. In this greatly needed new book, author Lynn M. Hamilton draws upon her own experience of successfully parenting an autistic child to give overwhelmed moms and dads guidance, practical information, and—best of all—hope for battling this disorder in their children's lives. In Facing Autism, parents will learn ten things they can do to begin battling autism right away, investigate cutting-edge biomedical treatments and other therapies, explore the benefits of dietary intervention, and much more as they learn how to begin the fight for their child's future.

Title: The New Social Story Book : Illustrated Edition
Author(s): Carol Gray
Miscellaneous Information: Paperback—120 pages 2nd ill edition (September 2000) Future Horizons; ISBN: 188547766X
Brief Description: The newest offering by Carol Gray. Social Stories help the child with autism or Asperger's Syndrome to understand the social world around them. This book is an updated version of the New Social Story Book with new text and accompanying illustrations.

Title: The OASIS Guide to Asperger Syndrome: Advice, Support, Insight, and Inspiration
Author(s): Patricia Romanowski Bashe, Barbara L. Kirby, Tony AttwoodForeword
Miscellaneous Information: Hardcover—467 pages 1st edition (November 13, 2001) Crown Pub; ISBN: 0609608118
Brief Description: As a parent of a boy diagnosed with AS in 1994, Barbara Kirby found scant resources and support. She developed the award-winning OASIS (Online Asperger Syndrome Information and Support) Web site in 1995 to help other parents find the information they need. She teamed up with Patricia Romanowski Bashe, now co-owner of OASIS and herself the

mother of a son with AS, to write The OASIS Guide to Asperger Syndrome, the most complete resource for parents and teachers of children with AS.

Title: The Out-Of-Sync Child : Recognizing and Coping With Sensory Integration Dysfunction
Author(s): Carol Stock Kranowitz, Larry B. Silver (Foreword)
Miscellaneous Information: Paperback—322 pages (March 1998) Perigee; ISBN: 0399523863
Brief Description: Do you know a child who plays too rough, is uncoordinated, hates being touched, is ultra-sensitive (or unusually insensitive) to noise or sensations of heat and cold? Many pediatricians and other experts are beginning to recognize a link between some of these apparently unrelated behavior patterns. Children with perfectly normal "far senses" (such as sight and hearing) may have, because of a poorly integrated nervous system, serious problems with their "near senses," including touch, balance, and internal muscle sensation. It's called Sensory Integration Dysfunction, or SI. The announcement of yet another new syndrome is bound to raise skeptical eyebrows—and with good reason. (How do we know which child really has SI, and which one just happens to share some of the same symptoms?) Author Carol Stock Kranowitz argues convincingly, however, that for some children SI is a real disorder, and that it is devastating partly because it so often looks like nothing so much as "being difficult." And, whatever the scientific status of SI, Kranowitz carefully details many routines and remedies that will help children—and the parents of children— who exhibit the behaviors described. This book is a must-read for all doctors, pediatricians, and (perhaps especially) childcare workers.

Title: Asperger Syndrome and Adolescence: Practical Solutions for School Success
Author(s): Brenda Smith Myles, Diane Adreon
Miscellaneous Information: Paperback—227 pages (May 17, 2001) Autism Asperger Publishing Co; ISBN: 0967251494
Brief Description: In this comprehensive book, the authors start with an overview of those characteristics of Asperger Syndrome that make adolescence particularly challenging and difficult. The

centerpiece of the book is a detailed discussion of strategies and supports necessary to ensure a successful school experience for students with Asperger Syndrome at the middle and secondary levels.

Title: Biological Treatments for Autism and PDD
Author(s): William Shaw
Miscellaneous Information: Paperback—225 pages (October 1, 2001) Great Plains Laboratory Inc; ISBN: 0966123816
Brief Description: Biological Treatments for Autism and PDD is an authoritative, comprehensive, and easy-to-read resource guide to a wide range of therapies that have been useful in the treatment of autism including antifungal and antibacterial therapies, gluten and casein restriction, homeopathy, vitamin therapy, gamma globulin treatment, transfer factor therapies, treatment of food allergies, and alternatives to antibiotic therapy. The information in this book may be useful not only in the field of autism but also in virtually any disorder in which some of the symptoms of autism are sometimes or frequently present.

Title: Asperger Syndrome and Difficult Moments: Practical Solutions for Tantrums, Rage, and Meltdowns
Author(s): Brenda Smith Myles, Jack Southwick
Miscellaneous Information: Paperback—107 pages (June 1999) Autism Asperger Publishing Co; ISBN: 0967251435
Brief Description: Written for professionals and parents alike, Asperger Syndrome and Rage: Practical Solutions for a Difficult Moment offers practical solutions to the day-to-day challenges facing individuals with Asperger Syndrome and their families. With a major emphasis on tantrums and other behavioral outbursts, the book offers strategies that promote social skills development, including self-awareness, self-calming and self-management thereby promoting effective lifelong practices. Solutions for parents include organization and support, the importance of daily routines, signs to watch for and more. This clear and concise discussion of the rage cycle and what can be done to stop it from escalating offers helpful suggestions designed to help children and youth function more successfully both at home and at school.

Title: Asperger's: What Does It Mean to Me?

Author(s): Catherine Faherty, Gary, Dr Mesibov, Gary B. Mesibov

Miscellaneous Information: Hardcover—301 pages Spiral edition (April 1, 2000) Future Horizons; ISBN: 1885477597

Brief Description: A workbook explaining self-awareness and life lessons to the youth with high functioning autism or Asperger's Syndrome. This is the book most requested by parents and teachers. Written by a leading therapist, this book is a must-have for the person with high functioning autism or Asperger's Syndrome. Includes chapters to help explain their world.

Title: Your Life is Not a Label: A Guide to Living Fully with Autism and Asperger's Syndrome

Author(s): Jerry Newport, Ron Bass

Miscellaneous Information: Paperback—317 pages (September 2001) Future Horizons; ISBN: 1885477775

Brief Description: An encouraging, educational, and often humorous guide for teens and young adults with Asperger's Syndrome or high-functioning autism. Jerry, a man with autism, gives advice on dating, money, traveling independently and more! This clever book will help others live fuller, more independent lives.

Learning Disabilities

Title: The Gift of Dyslexia : Why Some of the Smartest People Can't Read and How They Can Learn

Author(s): Ronald D. Davis, Eldon M. Braun (Contributor), Joan M. Smith

Miscellaneous Information: Paperback—258 pages (April 1997) Perigee; ISBN: 039952293X

Brief Description: The author shares the startling discovery that enabled him to overcome his own dyslexia, reveals how dyslexia can be related to high levels of intelligence, and offers a plan that anyone with dyslexia can use to conquer the common disability.

Title: THE LCP SOLUTION: The Remarkable Nutritional Treatment for ADHD, Dyslexia, and Dyspraxia

Author(s): B. Jacqueline, Ph.D. Stordy, Malcolm J. Nicholl, Jacqueline Stordy

Miscellaneous Information: Paperback—339 pages (September 5, 2000) Ballantine Books (Trd Pap); ISBN: 0345438728

Brief Description: In The LCP Solution, Dr. Stordy documents how this life-changing treatment came about and explains step-by-step how sufferers of each of the three major conditions can use it to change their lives at home, at school, and at work. Illuminating, vividly presented, and authoritative in its findings, this book will revolutionize our approach to learning disabilities. LCPs are natural, simple to use, and amazing in their benefits. If you or someone you love suffers from a learning disability, this book is essential reading.

Title: Postsecondary Education for Students With Learning Disabilities : A Handbook for Practitioners

Author(s): Loring Cowles Brinckerhoff, Joan McGuire, Stan F. Shaw

Miscellaneous Information: Hardcover 2nd edition (May 2002) Pro Ed; ISBN: 0890798729

Title: Multisensory Teaching of Basic Language Skills

Author(s): Judith R. Birsh (Editor)

Miscellaneous Information: Hardcover—608 pages (September 1999) Paul H Brookes Pub Co; ISBN: 1557663491

Brief Description: Comprehensive and practical, this guide reveals the benefits of using multisensory instruction in any classroom. After they review 50 years of research and clinical experience with children and adults with learning disabilities, the contributing authors explain how and why multisensory methods work.

Title: Learning Disabilities and Challenging Behaviors : A Guide to Intervention and Classroom Management

Author(s): Sam Goldstein, Nancy, Mather

Miscellaneous Information: Paperback—416 pages (June 1, 2001) Paul H Brookes Pub Co; ISBN: 1557665001

Brief Description: The Building Blocks model is practical, supported by research, and easy to implement. It identifies ten areas important to school success (the building blocks), divided into three levels: the foundational level includes attention and impulse control, emotion and behavior, self-esteem, and learning environment blocks the symbolic processing and memory level contains the visual, auditory, and motor skills blocks the conceptual level comprises using strategies and thinking with language and images.

Title: The Achievement Test Desk Reference: Comprehensive Assessment and Learning Disabilities
Author(s): Dawn P. Flanagan, Samuel O. Ortiz, Vincent C. Alfonso, Jennifer T. Mascolo
Miscellaneous Information: Hardcover 1st edition (December 3, 2001) Allyn & Bacon; ISBN: 0205325475
Brief Description: This book combines comprehensive descriptions and critical reviews of over 50 achievement tests with an innovative model for learning disability evaluation following current assessment and interpretation methods. The Achievement Test Desk Reference (ATDR) represents a unique contribution to both the practice of academic assessment and learning disability evaluation. The "Desk Reference" section contains descriptions and reviews of psychometric properties for comprehensive screening and specific academic skills batteries and achievement tests including measures of reading, math, written and oral language, and phonological processing. For school psychologists, clinical psychologists, educational psychologists, learning disability specialists, and speech/language pathologists.

Title: College and Career Success for Students With Learning Disabilities
Author(s): Roslyn Dolber
Miscellaneous Information: Paperback (April 1996) McGraw Hill— NTC; ISBN: 0844244791
Brief Description: This welcome guide helps learning-disabled students tackle all the critical issues of college and career. Tracing the many steps in the college assessment and application process with an eye to the special needs of this group, the book covers finding and gaining admission to the right college, preparing cover letters and resumes, exploring career options through networking and interviewing, evaluating job offers, and more.

Title: The Human Side of Dyslexia: 142 Interviews with Real People Telling Real Stories

Author(s): Shirley Kurnoff

Miscellaneous Information: Paperback—354 pages (November 5, 2001) London Universal Publishing; ISBN: 0970355726

Brief Description: An inside look into dyslexia—the challenges, emotions and rewards—from childhood through the college-experience. 142 interviews with families—parents, siblings and college students—sharing their experiences.

Title: How to Reach & Teach Children & Teens With Dyslexia

Author(s): Cynthia M. Stowe

Miscellaneous Information: Paperback—340 pages (August 2000) Center for Applied Research in Education; ISBN: 0130320188

Brief Description: This comprehensive, practical resource gives educators at all levels essential information, techniques, and tools for understanding dyslexia and adapting teaching methods in all subject areas to meet the learning style, social, and emotional needs of students who have dyslexia. Special features include over 50 full-page activity sheets that can be photocopied for immediate use and interviews with students and adults who have had personal experience with dyslexia. Organized into twenty sections, information covers everything from ten principles of instruction to teaching reading, handwriting, spelling, writing, math, everyday skills, and even covers the adult with dyslexia.

Title: To Teach a Dyslexic

Author(s): Don McCabe

Miscellaneous Information: Paperback—288 pages (May 1997) A V K O Educational Research; ISBN: 1564000044

Brief Description: Don McCabe writes a compelling autobiography to illustrate what it is like to grow up dyslexic. He was born in 1932 and this was well before dyslexia" was a term, let alone a diagnosis. He was just treated as a boy who couldn't sit still. He credits his older sister and wonderful teachers who worked intensively with him to help him learn to read and eventually to become a respected scholar. McCabe has dedicated the last thirty years to working on literacy. This book is a quick, fun read that shows a good dose of humor helps in discussing serious topics such as dyslexia. If you or someone you love has been diagnosed as dyslexic, don't wring your hands in despair—buy this book and learn from someone who knows firsthand about what it means to be a dyslexic.

Title: Dyslexia My Life
Author(s): Gigi Lane (Editor), Girard Sagmiller
Miscellaneous Information:
Brief Description: DYSLEXIA MY LIFE—one man's story of his life with a learning disability. In elementary school Girard Sagmiller was diagnosed as mentally retarded by his teacher and school administrators, who recommended that his family institutionalize him. In reality he suffered from dyslexia, which can affect speech, reading, time perception, and can slow learning in some subjects. In his book, DYSLEXIA MY LIFE, Girard Sagmiller discusses his struggles to overcome the ignorance and prejudice of his friends, family and society in general, to succeed in school (getting his MBA), business and life. The book DYSLEXIA MY LIFE has fairly large-size print and is packed full of emotion, drama, helpful tips, surprise and inspiration. It is told in the matter-of-fact tone of someone who has lived through quite extraordinary events without realizing they are anything out of ordinary. Besides being an engaging personal story, the book provides quite an education regarding the profound effects of dyslexia on a person's educational, social and emotional experiences.

Title: The Dyslexic Scholar : Helping Your Child Succeed in the School System
Author(s): Kathleen Nosek
Miscellaneous Information: Paperback—177 pages (April 1995) Taylor Pub; ISBN: 0878338829
Brief Description: Veteran educator Kathleen Nosek tells parents the secrets to successfully navigating today's school system and ensuring that dyslexic children receive the quality education they are entitled to by law. Includes a definition of dyslexia, how to identify it, how to get your child evaluated and more.

Title: Dyslexia In Adults: A Practical Guide for Working and Learning
Author(s): Gavin Reid, Jane Kirk, Gavin Reed
Miscellaneous Information: Paperback 1st edition (February 15, 2001) John Wiley & Sons; ISBN: 0471852058

Brief Description: More and more adults are being diagnosed with dyslexia, but little is available to help them. This book fills the gap by offering a comprehensive guide for professionals to working with adults with dyslexia in the learning and working environment.

Title: How to Reach & Teach Children & Teens With Dyslexia
Author(s): Cynthia M. Stowe
Miscellaneous Information: Paperback—340 pages (August 2000) Center for Applied Research in Education; ISBN: 0130320188
Brief Description: This comprehensive, practical resource gives educators at all levels essential information, techniques, and tools for understanding dyslexia and adapting teaching methods in all subject areas to meet the learning style, social, and emotional needs of students who have dyslexia. Special features include over 50 full-page activity sheets that can be photocopied for immediate use and interviews with students and adults who have had personal experience with dyslexia. Organized into twenty sections, information covers everything from ten principles of instruction to teaching reading, handwriting, spelling, writing, math, everyday skills, and even covers the adult with dyslexia.

Title: In the Mind's Eye: Visual Thinkers, Gifted People With Dyslexia and Other Learning Difficulties, Computer Images and the Ironies of Creativity
Author(s): Thomas G. West
Miscellaneous Information: Hardcover—395 pages Updated edition (September 1997) Prometheus Books; ISBN: 1573921556
Brief Description: In the Mind's Eye was selected as one of the "Outstanding Academic Books of 1998" by Choice magazine, a publication of the Association of College & Research Libraries of the American Library Association. In January 1999, the book was designated as among the "best of the best" for 1998, being among 13 books in the psychology category recommended for inclusion in college and university libraries.

Title: Dysgraphia : Why Johnny Can't Write : A Handbook for Teachers and Parents

Author(s): Diane Walton Cavey
Miscellaneous Information: Paperback 3rd edition (January 2000) Pro Ed; ISBN: 9990635625
Brief Description: This book provides lots of practical suggestions on how to maintain the self-esteem of children who struggle with writing.

Title: Eli, The Boy Who Hated To Write: Understanding Dysgraphia
Author(s): Regina G. Richards, Eli I. Richards, Judy Love (Illustrator), Lynn Craven (Illustrator)
Miscellaneous Information: Mass Market Paperback—96 pages (December 1, 2000) ISBN: 0966135334
Brief Description: Dysgraphia is often misunderstood by parents, teachers, and students. This book is designed to present a student's view of the struggles and frustrations, while also presenting hope and specific strategies and compensations. Students (particularly elementary and middle school ages) will enjoy reading about Eli's adventures. Parents and professionals will gain insight into some of the issues, particularly feelings, students may have related to having a significant writing problem, dysgraphia. Throughout the story, Eli describes his feelings about the issue of writing and the reactions of his peers and teachers. After a significant adventure, Eli and his friends realize that everyone is different with different combinations of strengths and weaknesses. Several appendices include actual stories written by Eli in elementary school and a list of specific strategies for students with writing problems. An epilogue presents an Allegory written by Eli in college.

Title: Unblocked! Dysgraphia Workbook : Clinical Curriculum
Author(s): Eve Engelbrite, Stone Engelbrite
Miscellaneous Information: Spiral-bound—112 pages (December 20, 2000) Inspired Idea; ISBN: 1931203024
Brief Description: Unblocked! contains letter-box grids onto which dysgraphic students trace and copy straight-line letters and numerals. It begins with single letters and words, and progresses to sentences and classic quotations. Transitional pages at the end ease the student into writing on normal, lined paper.

Behavior Disorders

Title: Skills Training for Children with Behavior Disorders

Author(s): Michael L. Bloomquist

Miscellaneous Information: Paperback—272 pages 1st edition (March 8, 1996) Guilford Press; ISBN: 1572300809

Brief Description: Presents detailed strategies for parents and therapists working with behavior-disordered children, offering background information on the disorders, step-by-step instructions, concrete examples, and worksheets. A parent section overviews the nature of behavior disorders and common treatment approaches, and shows how to evaluate which areas the child and family need to work on most. A therapist section delineates the theoretical underpinnings of the author's approach, and details procedures for conducting skills training.

Title: Cognitive-Behavioral Treatment of Borderline Personality Disorder

Author(s): Marsha M. Linehan

Miscellaneous Information: Hardcover—558 pages (May 14, 1993) Guilford Press; ISBN: 0898621836

Brief Description: These two companion volumes are an impressive summary of Marsha Linehan's work which is increasingly well-known on both sides of the Atlantic. The book is also an encyclopedia of all problems ever encountered with borderline patients, offering usually well thought-out therapeutic strategies.

Title: Pediatric Disorders of Regulation in Affect and Behavior: A Therapist's Guide to Assessment and Treatment (Practical Resources for the Mental Health Professional)

Author(s): Georgia A. DeGangi

Miscellaneous Information: Paperback—316 pages (July 2000) Academic Pr; ISBN: 0122087704

Brief Description: Pediatric Disorders of Regulation in Affect and Behavior: A Therapist's Guide to Assessment and Treatment represents state of the art coverage of the latest theory, research and treatment strategies for infants and children with problems of regulation. This comprehensive book, designed for mental health professionals and occupational therapists working with infants and children, provides the most recent advances in addressing disorders of self-regulation.

Title: Transforming the Difficult Child: The Nurtured Heart Approach
Author(s): Howard Glasser, Jennifer Easley
Miscellaneous Information: Paperback—250 pages (April 1999) Children's Success Foundation; ISBN: 0967050707
Brief Description: Transforming the Difficult Child brings to life a new way of shifting intense children to a solid life of success. The Nurtured Heart Approach puts a refreshing spin on both parenting and teaching and reveals new techniques and strategies that create thoroughly positive behaviors.

Title: The Explosive Child: A New Approach for Understanding and Parenting Easily Frustrated, Chronically Inflexible Children
Author(s): Ross W. Greene
Miscellaneous Information: Paperback—352 pages 2nd edition (January 23, 2001) HarperCollins; ISBN: 0060931027
Brief Description: An explosive child who frequently exhibits severe noncompliance, temper outbursts, and verbal or physical aggression. If this sounds like your child, you're probably feeling frustrated, guilt-ridden, and overwhelmed. At last, Dr. Ross Greene offers help for you and your child. Now updated with new practical information, The Explosive Child lays out a sensitive, practical approach to helping your child at home and school, including: reducing hostility and antagonism between the child and adults anticipating situations in which the child is most likely to explode creating an environment in which explosions are less likely to occur focusing less on reward and punishment and more on communication and collaborating problem solving helping your child develop the skills to be more flexible and handle frustration more adaptively

Title: Surviving Manic Depression: A Manual on Bipolar Disorder for Patients, Families, and Providers
Author(s): E. Fuller Torrey, Michael B. Knable
Miscellaneous Information: Hardcover—416 pages 1st edition (January 8, 2002) Basic Books; ISBN: 0465086632
Brief Description: Surviving Manic Depression is the most authoritative book on this disorder, which affects more than two million people in the U.S. alone. Based on the latest research, it provides detailed coverage of every aspect of manic depression—from understanding its causes and treatments to choosing doctors and

managing relapses—with guidance drawn from the latest scientific information.

Title: Brain Lock : Free Yourself from Obsessive-Compulsive Behavior : A Four-Step Self-Treatment Method to Change Your Brain Chemistry

Author(s): Jeffrey M. Schwartz, Beverly Beyette (Contributor)

Miscellaneous Information: Paperback—219 pages (March 1997) HarperCollins (paper); ISBN: 0060987111

Brief Description: An estimated 5 million Americans suffer from obsessive-compulsive disorder (OCD) and live diminished lives in which they are compelled to obsess about something or to repeat a similar task over and over. Traditionally, OCD has been treated with Prozac or similar drugs. The problem with medication, aside from its cost, is that 30 percent of people treated don't respond to it, and when the pills stop, the symptoms invariably return.

Title: Mind Over Mood

Author(s): Dennis Greenberger, Christine A. Padesky

Miscellaneous Information: Paperback—243 pages 1st edition (March 28, 1995) Guilford Press; ISBN: 0898621283

Brief Description: Ideal for client assignment, this treatment manual draws on the authors' extensive experience as clinicians and teachers of cognitive therapy to help clients successfully understand and improve their moods, alter their behavior, and enhance their relationships.

Title: Overcoming Binge Eating

Author(s): Christopher Fairburn

Miscellaneous Information: Paperback—247 pages Reissue edition (March 10, 1995) Guilford Press; ISBN: 0898621798

Brief Description: Proven Effective in Clinical Research! Do you have a binge eating problem or know someone who does? This authoritative book provides all the information needed to understand binge eating and bring it under control. Whether you are working with a therapist or on your own, clear, step-by-step guidelines will show you how to: overcome the urge to binge, gain control over eating behavior, reduce the risk of relapse, establish stable, and healthy eating habits.

Title: Characteristics of Emotional and Behavioral Disorders of Children and Youth
Author(s): James M. Kauffman
Miscellaneous Information: Hardcover—624 pages 7 edition (July 26, 2000) Prentice Hall; ISBN: 0130832839
Brief Description: This book, like its earlier editions, serves primarily as an introductory text in special education for children and youth with emotional and behavioral disorders (those called "emotionally disturbed' in federal regulations). Because emotional and behavioral disorders are commonly observed in children and youth in all special education categories, the book will also be of value in courses dealing with the characteristics of mental retardation, learning disabilities, or students in cross-categorical special education. Students in school psychology, educational psychology, or abnormal child psychology may also find the book useful.

Title: Conduct Disorders in Childhood and Adolescence
Author(s): Jonathan Hill (Editor), Barbara Maughan (Editor)
Miscellaneous Information: Paperback—416 pages 1st edition (December 15, 2000) Cambridge University Press; ISBN: 0521786398
Brief Description: Highlights the complexity and probable heterogeneity of the condition. For mental health practitioners and others with clinical, sociological or medicolegal interests in child health and behavior.

Title: Complete Early Childhood Behavior Management Guide
Author(s): Kathleen Pullan Watkins, Lucius Durant
Miscellaneous Information: Hardcover—192 pages (August 1992) Center for Applied Research in Education; ISBN: 0876282613
Brief Description: Includes practical techniques and ready-to-use materials to help early childhood educators promote good behavior in children from birth to age nine, with strategies for handling a broad range of behavior problems in any early childhood setting. Includes forms, checklists and quizzes for individuals and staffs.

Title: Disruptive Behavior Disorders Children Disruptive Behavior Disorders in Children and Adolescents
Author(s): Robert L. Hendren (Editor)

Miscellaneous Information: Paperback—198 pages 1st edition Vol 18 (May 15, 1999) Amer Psychiatric Pr; ISBN: 088048960X

Brief Description: Robert Johnson Medical School, Piscataway, NJ. Reviews current research and clinical observations on the topic. Discusses attention-deficit/hyperactivity disorder, conduct disorder, and oppositional defiant disorder. For clinicians and therapists.

Title: Antisocial Behavior in School: Strategies and Best Practices

Author(s): Geoff Colvin, Elizabeth Ramsey, Hill M. Ramsey Walker

Miscellaneous Information: Paperback—480 pages 1st edition (November 8, 1994) Wadsworth Pub Co; ISBN: 0534256449

Brief Description: This indispensable resource describes the "best practices" for coping with antisocial behavior patterns among children and youth in school. Designed to enhance educators' understanding of the nature, origins, and causes of antisocial behavior, this book offers interventions and model programs that can be used in preventing or remediating this growing problem in the schools.

Title: Survival Strategies For Parenting Children With Bipolar Disorder: Innovative Parenting And Counseling Techniques For Helping Children With Bipolar Disorder And The Conditions That May Occur With It

Author(s): George T. Lynn

Miscellaneous Information: Paperback—240 pages (September 2000) Jessica Kingsley Pub; ISBN: 1853029211

Brief Description: Up until five years ago, the professional community did not think that Bipolar Disorder occurred in children. Children with symptoms of Bipolar Disorder were diagnosed as 'severe ADHD', 'depressed' or 'Oppositional Defiant'. Now, as it is being increasingly diagnosed, George Lynn offers clear, practical advice on recognizing the symptoms, understanding medication and accessing the necessary support at school as well as the managing the day-to-day challenges of parenting a child with Bipolar Disorder. As it is frequently found in combination with ADHD, Tourette Syndrome and Asperger's Syndrome, the author draws on case-studies from his own psychotherapeutic practice to show what these conditions have in common, how they differ, and how they relate to each other.

Title: When Nothing Matters Anymore : A Survival Guide for Depressed Teens

Author(s): Bev Cobain, Elizabeth Verdick (Editor), Jeff Tolbert (Illustrator)

Miscellaneous Information: Paperback—176 pages (July 1998) Free Spirit Publishing; ISBN: 1575420368

Brief Description: A guide to understanding and coping with depression, discussing the different types, how and why the condition begins, how it may be linked to substance abuse or suicide, and how to get help.

Attention Deficit Hyperactivity Disorders

Title: Teaching Superman How To Fly: Making ADHD A Gift

Author(s): Robert Evert Cimera

Miscellaneous Information: (2002) Scarecrow Education Press

Brief Description: This book provides an easy-to-read overview of what ADHD is and current thoughts as to what causes it. It also provides several chapters of useful strategies for making ADHD a positive condition to have.

Title: Taking Charge of ADHD, Revised Edition

Author(s): Russell A. Barkley

Miscellaneous Information: Paperback—321 pages Revised edition (September 1, 2000) Guilford Press; ISBN: 1572305606

Brief Description: Taking Charge of ADHD is an outstanding resource for parents of children with the syndrome currently known as Attention Deficit Hyperactivity Disorder. In this book, Dr. Barkley and his colleagues have integrated their great compassion for families with the scientific authority for which they are known. Dr. Barkley guides parents in examining their foundational beliefs about parenthood, the nature of ADHD, and the principles and priorities that guide their actions. When he issues challenges, they are accompanied by advice and tools.

Title: How to Reach and Teach ADD/ADHD Children : Practical Techniques, Strategies, and Interventions for Helping Children With Attention Problems and Hyperactivity

Author(s): Sandra F. Rief

Miscellaneous Information: Paperback—256 pages (March 1993) Center for Applied Research in Education; ISBN: 0876284136

Brief Description: A comprehensive resource that addresses the "whole child," as well as the team approach to meeting the needs of students with attention deficit hyperactivity disorder. Includes management techniques that promote on-task behavior and language arts, whole language, and multi-sensory instruction strategies that maintain student attention and keep students involved.

Title: No More ADHD

Author(s): Mary Ann Block

Miscellaneous Information: Paperback—178 pages Updated edition (May 11, 2001) Block Books; ISBN: 0966554531

Brief Description: In her new book, No More ADHD, 10 Steps To Help Improve Your Child's Attention and Behavior without Drugs, Dr. Mary Ann Block, top-selling author of the groundbreaking book, No More Ritalin, reveals the truth about the ADHD diagnosis and helps parents, step by step identify and improve their child's true health and learning problems. Dr. Block takes the reader on a shocking journey behind the scenes of the medical profession to expose the origin of the ADHD label and explains how children's attention and behavior symptoms can be the result of real and explainable health and learning problems.

Title: ADHD : A Path to Success—A Revolutionary Theory and New Innovation in Drug-Free Therapy

Author(s): Lawrence Weathers, Kelsey Loughlin (Illustrator)

Miscellaneous Information: Paperback—313 pages (June 1998) Ponderosa Pr; ISBN: 0965951316

Brief Description: Most books on ADHD rehash the same worn-out theories and treatments. Instead, ADHD: A Path to Success offers a new perspective on ADHD that makes sense with your own personal experience.—it is not a deficit, defect or neurological disorder.

Title: The Down & Dirty Guide to Adult ADD

Author(s): Michael Gordon

Miscellaneous Information: Paperback (January 1996) Gsi Pubns; ISBN: 0962770191

Title: Being In Control: Natural Techniques For Increasing Your Potential and Creativity For Success in School. Also For Improving Concentration and Learning in Children with ADHD and Dyslexia
Author(s): Jason Mark Alster
Miscellaneous Information: Paperback—40 pages (December 2001) Rainbow Cloud; ISBN: 9659025114
Brief Description: Being In control. Natural Techniques For Increasing Your Potential And Creativity For Success In School. Also For Improving Concentration And Learning In Children With ADHD And Dyslexia.

Title: Jumpin' Johnny Get Back to Work! : A Child's Guide to ADHD/Hyperactivity
Author(s): Michael Gordon Ph.D.
Miscellaneous Information: Paperback (December 1991) Gsi Pubns; ISBN: 0962770116

Title: I Would If I Could : A Teenagers Guide ADHD Hyperactive
Author(s): Michael Gordon
Miscellaneous Information: Paperback (November 1992) Gsi Pubns; ISBN: 0962770132

Physical Disabilities

Title: Si for Early Intervention: A Team Approach
Author(s): Katherine Newton Inamura (Editor), Shay McAtee (Photographer)
Miscellaneous Information: Paperback—214 pages 1st edition (January 15, 1998) Therapy Skill Builders; ISBN: 0127845992
Brief Description: This book presents an example of a sensory integration-based early intervention program that uses a team approach and has been the model for programs elsewhere. No doubt the contents of this 214-page professional resource will prove to be invaluable to occupational and physical therapists who read them.

Title: Extraordinary People With Disabilities (Extraordinary People)
Author(s): Deborah Kent, Kathryn A. Quinlan (Contributor)
Miscellaneous Information: Paperback—256 pages (April 1997) Children's Press; ISBN: 051626074X

Brief Description: This book profiles over fifty notable figures, both historic and contemporary, who have dealt with disabilities such as blindness, autism, and paraplegia. Written in flat prose and illustrated with black-and-white photographs, the biographical essays contain inspiring elements but are sometimes incomplete in content. The book also includes a handful of articles on disability-related topics.

Title: Caring for People With Multiple Disabilities : An Interdisciplinary Guide for Caregivers
Author(s): Cindy French, Robin Tapp Gonzalez, Jan Tronson-Simpson
Miscellaneous Information: Paperback—145 pages (January 1998) Psychological Corp; ISBN: 0127845550

Title: Children With Cerebral Palsy : A Parents' Guide
Author(s): Elaine Geralis (Editor)
Miscellaneous Information: Paperback—481 pages 2nd edition (September 1998) Woodbine House; ISBN: 0933149824
Brief Description: A revised and updated edition of this classic primer for parents provides a complete spectrum of information and compassionate advice about cerebral palsy and its effect on their child's development and education.

Title: Cerebral Palsy : A Complete Guide for Caregiving
Author(s): Freeman Miller, Steven J. Bachrach
Miscellaneous Information: Paperback—488 pages Reprint edition (April 1998) Johns Hopkins Univ Pr; ISBN: 0801859492
Brief Description: A guide for parents and caregivers of children and adults with cerebral palsy (CP), as well as for adolescents and adults with the condition. Part I provides an overview of CP and explains the medical and psychosocial implications of associated conditions, offering advice for parents on becoming an advocate for their child. Part II contains practical information on caregiving and medical procedures. Part III defines and describes medical terms and diagnoses, surgical procedures, and assistive devices. Includes a list of resources and recommended reading.

Title: My Perfect Son Has Cerebral Palsy : A Mother's Guide of Helpful Hints
Author(s): Marie A. Kennedy

Miscellaneous Information: Paperback—108 pages (February 2001) 1st Books Library; ISBN: 0759609543

Title: Posture and Movement of the Child With Cerebral Palsy
Author(s): Marcia H. Stamer
Miscellaneous Information: Paperback—252 pages (June 2001) Academic Pr; ISBN: 0127844708

Title: Howie Helps Himself.
Author(s): Joan Fassler, Joe Lasker (Illustrator)
Miscellaneous Information: School & Library Binding—32 pages (September 1987) Albert Whitman & Co; ISBN: 0807534226

Title: Caring for Children with Cerebral Palsy: A Teambased Approach
Author(s): John P. Dormans (Editor), Louis Pellegrino (Editor)
Miscellaneous Information: Paperback—533 pages 1st edition (January 15, 1998) Paul H Brookes Pub Co; ISBN: 155766322X
Brief Description: An interdisciplinary reference for team-based, collaborative care of children with cerebral palsy. Twenty-one chapters detail information on diagnosis, management of impairments, optimizing function and preventing disability, and preventing handicap by creating opportunities. They address family, school, and community roles as well as law and public policy

Title: Spinal Cord Injury: A Guide for Living
Author(s): Sara Palmer, Kay Harris, Ph.D. Kriegsman, Jeffrey B., M.D. Palmer
Miscellaneous Information: Paperback—290 pages 1st edition (May 15, 2000) Johns Hopkins Univ Pr; ISBN: 0801863538
Brief Description: Designed to help those with spinal cord injuries, their families, and friends, during the rehabilitation process. Reviews the challenges that may be encountered throughout their lives. Illustrated chapters with patient stories are included.

Title: The Child With a Spinal Cord Injury
Author(s): Randal R. Betz (Editor), M. J. Mulcahey (Editor)
Miscellaneous Information: Paperback (February 1996) Amer Academy of Orthopaedic; ISBN: 0892031468

Brief Description: Aims to provide a contemporary review of pediatric SCIs in order to disseminate standards for optimal care of affected children and adolescents, identify areas of deficient knowledge, and encourage research. Contains 68 contributions in sections on etiology and prevention, management, medical issues, orthopedic problems, upper extremity management, rehabilitation, discharge and transition, habilitation, research and technological applications, and special considerations.

Sensory Impairments

Title: Dancing in the Dark : A Guide to Living With Blindness and Visual Impairment
Author(s): Frances Lief Neer
Miscellaneous Information: Paperback—128 pages (November 1994) Wildstar Pub; ISBN: 0963783904
Brief Description: A direct, good-humored, non-threatening reference guide for living in a frightening situation. It is for people affected personally as well as professionally. Dancing in the Dark includes a resource directory and primer to understand the language of visual impairment.

Title: Technology for All: Assistive Technology in the Classroom
Author(s): OSB Staff
Miscellaneous Information: Spiral-bound—160 pages (October 1, 2001) Towers Press, Overbrook School for the Blind; ISBN: 1930526016
Brief Description: This 160-page book is an easy-to-read, field tested resource for all schools and colleges that need assistive technology in the classroom. Technology for All: Assistive Technology in the Classroom is written by the educational staff who developed Overbrook 2001—the nationally recognized schoolwide technology project—and by teachers who use access technology every day.

Title: Living With Vision Problems : The Blindness and Vision Impairment Sourcebook (The Facts for Life Series)
Author(s): Jill Sardegna (Editor), Susan Shelly, Allan Rutzen, Scott M. Steidl

Miscellaneous Information: Paperback—256 pages (July 1, 2002) Checkmark Books; ISBN: 0816042810

Brief Description: Living with Vision Impairment is a complete personal reference to what has become one of the most common disabilities in the United States, offering key information on causes and prevention of vision problems, treatment options, living with vision impairment, and helping loved ones with vision impairment. Among topics covered are: living with blindness, how to cope with vision impairments, causes of blindness, types of vision impairment, treatments and prevention, and LASIK vision correction procedures.

Title: Low Vision : A Resource Guide With Adaptations for Students With Visual Impairments

Author(s): Nancy Levak, Gretchen Stone, Virginia E. Bishop

Miscellaneous Information: Spiral-bound 2nd edition (February 1994) Texas School for the Blind &; ISBN: 1880366126

Title: Deaf Like Me

Author(s): Thomas S. Spradley, James P. Spradley

Miscellaneous Information: Paperback—292 pages Reissue edition (May 1985) Gallaudet Univ Pr; ISBN: 0930323114

Title: Signing for Kids

Author(s): Mickey Flodin

Miscellaneous Information: Paperback—142 pages (June 1991) Perigee; ISBN: 0399516727

Brief Description: The first signing manual written for kids, this invaluable learning guide is created especially for eight to fourteen-year-olds. Presented in an easy-to-follow, more detailed, larger format, Signing for Kids is arranged by general subject area. Included among the subjects are: a manual alphabet; pets/animals; snacks/food; sports/school; family/friends; money/numbers, and much more. A helpful "How to Use This Book" section is also included.

Title: American Sign Language the Easy Way (Easy Way.)

Author(s): David Stewart

Miscellaneous Information: Paperback (July 1998) Barrons Educational Series; ISBN: 0764102990

Title: The Joy of Signing : The Illustrated Guide for Mastering Sign
   Language and the Manual Alphabet
Author(s): Lottie L. Riekehof
Miscellaneous Information: Hardcover—352 pages 2nd edition
   (May 1987) Gospel Pub House; ISBN: 0882435205
Brief Description: In this standard work on sign language for the
   deaf, over 1500 signs have been clearly illustrated and are grouped
   by chapter into their natural categories. Line drawings and step-
   by-step descriptions of hand positions aid rapid learning.

Gifted and Talented

Title: The Drama of the Gifted Child : The Search for the True Self
Author(s): Alice Miller, Ruth Ward (Translator)
Miscellaneous Information: Paperback—136 pages Rev&Updtd edition (December 1996) Basic Books; ISBN: 0465016901
Brief Description: As charming performers who skillfully reflect
   their parents expectations, far too many children grow into adults
   driven to greater and greater achievements by an underlying sense
   of worthlessness. Never allowed to express their true feelings, and
   having lost touch with their true selves, they act out their repressed
   feelings with episodes of depression and compulsive behavior.
   They in turn inflict the same legacy of repression on their own
   children. This poignant and thought-provoking book shows how
   narcissistic parents form and deform the lives of their children.
   The Drama of the Gifted Child is the first step toward helping
   readers reclaim their lives by discovering their own needs and their
   own truth.

Title: Teaching Gifted Kids in the Regular Classroom: Strategies and
   Techniques Every Teacher Can Use to Meet the Academic Needs
   of the Gifted and Talented (Revised and Updated Edition)
Author(s): Susan Winebrenner, Pamela Espeland (Editor)
Miscellaneous Information: Paperback—184 pages Rev&Updtd edi-
   tion (November 2000) Free Spirit Publishing; ISBN: 1575420899
Brief Description: With 150,000 copies in print, the original
   TEACHING GIFTED KIDS is a perennial best-seller. Teachers
   everywhere call it, "the orange Bible" and turn to it daily to make

sure their gifted students are getting the learning opportunities they need and deserve. Since the first edition was published, author Susan Winebrenner has spent eight years using it with school districts, teachers, parents, and kids across the U.S. and the U.K. This revised, expanded, updated edition reflects her personal experiences and the changes that have taken place in education over the years. Her basic philosophy hasn't changed, and all of the proven, practical, classroom-tested strategies teachers love are still here. But there's now an entire chapter on identifying gifted students. The step-by-step how-tos for using the strategies are more detailed and user-friendly. There's a new chapter especially for parents. And all of the forms in the book are also on CD-ROM (sold separately) so you can print them out and customize them for your classroom.

Title: Systems and Models for Developing Programs for the Gifted and Talented
Author(s): Joseph Renzulli
Miscellaneous Information: Paperback (August 1986) Creative Learning Pr; ISBN: 0936386444

Title: The Einstein Syndrome: Bright Children Who Talk Late
Author(s): Thomas Sowell
Miscellaneous Information: Hardcover—256 pages (August 21, 2001) Basic Books; ISBN: 0465081401
Brief Description: The Einstein Syndrome is a follow-up to Late-Talking Children, which established Thomas Sowell as a leading spokesman on the subject of late-talking children. While many children who talk late suffer from developmental disorders or autism, there is a certain well-defined group who are developmentally normal or even quite bright, yet who may go past their fourth birthday before beginning to talk. These children are often misdiagnosed as autistic or retarded, a mistake that is doubly hard on parents who must first worry about their apparently handicapped children and then see them lumped into special classes and therapy groups where all the other children are clearly very different.

Title: Gifted Grownups: The Mixed Blessings of Extraordinary Potential

Author(s): Marylou Kelly Streznewski

Miscellaneous Information: Hardcover—292 pages 1 edition (March 15, 1999) John Wiley & Sons; ISBN: 0471295809

Brief Description: Gifted Grownups, Marylou Kelly Streznewski's unprecedented, 10-year study of 100 gifted adults, examines how being identified as a "smart kid" early on affects career choices, friendships, and romantic pairings later in life. Why do some talented and gifted people become Mozarts and Einsteins or corporate chieftains, while others drop out of school, struggle to hold down jobs, or turn to self-destructive behavior? What are the signs of giftedness, its pitfalls, and its promise? Marylou Streznewski provides answers to these and other questions, and creates an intriguing picture of what it is like to have an accelerated mind in a slow-moving world.

Title: Dreamers, Discoverers and Dynamos : How to Help the Child Who Is Bright, Bored and Having Problems in School

Author(s): Lucy Jo Palladino

Miscellaneous Information: Paperback—336 pages (January 1999) Ballantine Books (Trd Pap); ISBN: 0345405730

Brief Description: With many references to scientific studies, Palladino helps you decide whether your child is one of the three types of Edison-trait children: dreamer, discoverer, or dynamo. She also gives pointed, practical advice regarding such controversial topics as diet, neurofeedback treatment, and psychological testing. For frustrated parents and educators, Dreamers, Discoverers, and Dynamos will be a rich source of both help and hope.

Title: The Gifted Kids' Survival Guide for Ages 10 & Under

Author(s): Judy Galbraith, Pamela Espeland, Albert Molnar (Illustrator)

Miscellaneous Information: Paperback—104 pages Rev expand edition (November 1998) Free Spirit Publishing; ISBN: 1575420538

Brief Description: First published in 1984, newly revised and updated, this book has helped countless young gifted children realize they're not alone and being smart, talented and creative is a bonus—not a burden. It answers their questions about why they think and learn the way they do, and what "giftedness" and IQ really mean, and how to handle high expectations.

Title: Talented Teenagers: The Roots of Success and Failure

Author(s): Mihaly Csikszentmihalyi, Kevin Rathunde, Samuel Whalen, Maria Wong (Contributor)

Miscellaneous Information: Paperback—320 pages Reprint edition (October 2000) Cambridge Univ Pr (Pap Txt); ISBN: 0521574633

Brief Description: The findings in this book are the results of a monumental five-year study of a group of exceptionally talented teenagers, examining the role that personality traits, family interactions, education, and the social environment play in a young person's motivation to develop his or her talent.

OTHER USEFUL RESOURCES

In this section, you can find additional resources on special education related topics, such as assistive technology, estate planning, and governmental agencies.

Assistive Technology Websites

ABLEDATA

www.abledata.com

ABLEDATA is a federally funded project whose primary mission is to provide information on assistive technology and rehabilitation equipment available from domestic and international sources to consumers, organizations, professionals, and caregivers within the United States.

Alliance for Technology Access (ATA)

www.ataccess.org

The Alliance for Technology Access (ATA) is a network of community-based Resource Centers, Developers and Vendors, Affiliates, and Associates dedicated to providing information and support services to children and adults with disabilities, and increasing their use of standard, assistive, and information technologies.

WebABLE!

www.webable.com

At WebABLE, our mission is to make the Internet, World Wide Web, and software accessible to people with disabilities. To accomplish this mission, we provide accessibility technology and services to corporate, government, educational, and non-profit clients.

Child Abuse Prevention and Resources

Child Abuse Prevention Network
www.child-abuse.com
The Child Abuse Prevention Network is the Internet Nerve Center for professionals in the field of child abuse and neglect. Child maltreatment, physical abuse, psychological maltreatment, neglect, sexual abuse, and emotional abuse and neglect are our key areas of concern. We provide unique and powerful tools for all workers to support the identification, investigation, treatment, adjudication, and prevention of child abuse and neglect.

Child Abuse Prevention Association
www.childabuseprevention.org
The mission of CAPA is to prevent and treat all forms of child abuse by creating changes in individuals, families and society, which strengthen relationships and promote healing.

National Data Archive on Child Abuse and Neglect
www.ndacan.cornell.edu
The mission of the National Data Archive on Child Abuse and Neglect (NDACAN) is to facilitate the secondary analysis of research data relevant to the study of child abuse and neglect. By making data available to a larger number of researchers, NDACAN seeks to provide a relatively inexpensive and scientifically productive means for researchers to explore important issues in the child maltreatment field.

PAVNET Online
www.pavnet.org
Partnerships Against Violence Network is a "virtual library" of information about violence and youth-at-risk, representing data from seven different Federal agencies.

Drug and Alcohol Abuse and Prevention

National Council on Alcoholism and Drug Dependence
www.ncadd.org
Founded in 1944 by Marty Mann, the first woman to find long-term sobriety in Alcoholics Anonymous, the National Council on Alcoholism

and Drug Dependence, Inc. (NCADD) provides education, information, help and hope to the public. It advocates prevention, intervention and treatment through offices in New York and Washington, and a nationwide network of Affiliates.

AL-ANON
www.al-anon.org

To help families and friends of alcoholics recover from the effects of living with the problem drinking of a relative or friend. Similarly, Alateen is our recovery program for young people. Alateen groups are sponsored by Al-Anon members.

AL-ALATEEN
www.al-anon.org/alateen.html

Al-Alateen is a fellowship of young Al-Anon members, usually teenagers, whose lives have been affected by someone else's drinking.

National Association for Children of Alcoholics
www.nacoa.net

The National Association for Children of Alcoholics (NACoA) believes that none of these vulnerable children should grow up in isolation and without support. NACoA is the national nonprofit membership organization working on behalf of children of alcohol and drug dependent parents.

Estate Planning

Future Planning Resources
www.thearc.org/misc/futplan.html

This website provides resources for planning for the future economic needs of children with disabilities.

Life Services for the Handicapped
www.disabledandalone.org

The purpose of Life Services for the Handicapped is to maintain the highest quality of life for each disabled member through the full utilization of private and government programs and parent funded supplemental services; to ensure that each disabled member pursues activities and associations which prevent isolation and loneliness; to preserve the full integrity of funds left by the family so that they may be used to enrich the life of the disabled individual, without jeopardizing public entitlements; and to provide families with peace of mind related to the future care of their disabled loved ones.

Federal Government Agencies

Department of Education
www.ed.gov
The U.S. Department of Education was established on May 4, 1980 by Congress in the Department of Education Organization Act (Public Law 96-88 of October 1979). The Department's mission is to strengthen the Federal commitment to assuring access to equal educational opportunity for every individual; supplement and complement the efforts of states, the local school systems and other instrumentalities of the states, the private sector, public and private nonprofit educational research institutions, community-based organizations, parents, and students to improve the quality of education; encourage the increased involvement of the public, parents, and students in Federal education programs, promote improvements in the quality and usefulness of education through Federally supported research, evaluation, and sharing of information, improve the coordination of Federal education programs; improve the management of Federal education activities; and increase the accountability of Federal education programs to the President, the Congress, and the public.

Office of Special Education and Rehabilitative Services (OSERS)
www.ed.gov/offices/OSERS
OSERS is committed to working with internal and external partners in ensuring that every individual with a disability maximizes their potential to participate in school, work, and community life. Recognizing our legacy of accomplishment, OSERS understands the many challenges still facing individuals with disabilities and their families. We are dedicated to identifying and using what works and collaborating with the scientific community to conduct and disseminate the highest quality research in areas where more knowledge is needed.

National Institute of Health (NIH)
www.nih.gov

The NIH mission is to uncover new knowledge that will lead to better health for everyone.

Social Security Online
www.ssa.gov
This website provides answers to frequently asked questions and other resources regarding social security services.

The Official U.S. Government Site for People with Medicare
www.medicare.gov
This website provides information and resources regarding medicare and its regulations.

Legal Resources and Advocacy Organizations

American Association of People with Disabilities
www.aapd-dc.org
We are over 50 million strong—People with disabilities in America, plus our families and friends. We see the need for one unifying membership organization to leverage the numbers of people with disabilities and their families and friends to access economic and other benefits to form an organization which will be a positive private-sector force to achieve the goal of full inclusion in American society.

Child Care Law Center
www.childcarelaw.org
CCLC's primary objective is to use legal tools to foster the development of high quality, affordable child care—for every child, every parent, every community. CCLC works to expand child care options, particularly for low income families, and to ensure that children are safe and nurtured in care outside the home.

Disability Rights Advocates
www.dralegal.org
Founded in 1993, Disability Rights Advocates is a national and international non-profit organization dedicated to protecting and advancing the civil rights of people with disabilities. Operated by and established for people with disabilities, DRA pursues its mission through research, education, and legal advocacy. DRA's mission is to ensure dignity,

equality, and opportunity for people with all types of disabilities throughout the United States and worldwide.

EDLAW, Inc.

www.edlaw.net

EDLAW has pioneered providing access to the texts of laws governing the provision of special education. We have invested additional effort to reformat the text of IDEA and some other materials to make them easier to read and use. However, for most texts, the time required is simply not available. In these situations, we have either used the formatted text as we discovered it or provided links to other sources.

American Bar Association

www.abanet.org

The ABA strives to provide you with the knowledge and tools you need to expand your career. From ABA-sponsored workshops, meetings, seminars and CLE sessions to the widest variety of respected and up-to-date publications, the ABA is your association, dedicated to helping you advance your career and the legal profession.

Disability Rights Education and Defense Fund, Inc.

www.dredf.org

Founded in 1979 by people with disabilities and parents of children with disabilities, the Disability Rights Education and Defense Fund, Inc. (DREDF) is a national law and policy center dedicated to protecting and advancing the civil rights of people with disabilities through legislation, litigation, advocacy, technical assistance, and education and training of attorneys, advocates, persons with disabilities, and parents of children with disabilities.

National Association of Protection and Advocacy Systems

www.protectionandadvocacy.com/napas.htm

NAPAS is a national voluntary membership organization for the federally mandated nationwide network of disability rights agencies, protection & advocacy systems (P&As), and client assistance programs (CAPs).

National Association for Rights Protection and Advocacy

www.connix.com/~narpa

NARPA is dedicated to promoting those policies and pursuing those strategies that represent the preferred options of people who have been labeled mentally disabled. NARPA is committed to advocating the abolishing of all forced treatment laws. NARPA believes the recipients of mental health services are capable of and entitled to make their own choices, and they are, above all, equal citizens under the law. To the extent that the recipients and former recipients may need assistance to support or express or achieving their preferences, NARPA is committed to promoting rights protection and advocacy which focuses upon both the right to choose and the specific choices of those who request assistance. Therefore, NARPA's fundamental mission is to help empower people who have been labeled mentally disabled so that they may learn to independently exercise their rights.

Parent Advocacy Coalition for Educational Rights (PACER)
www.pacer.org
The mission of PACER Center is to expand opportunities and enhance the quality of life of children and young adults with disabilities and their families, based on the concept of parents helping parents. With assistance to individual families, workshops, and materials for parents and professionals, and leadership in securing a free and appropriate public education for all children, PACER's work affects and encourages families in Minnesota and across the nation.

Summer Camps for Individuals with Disabilities

Kids Camps
www.kidscamps.com
This website lists numerous summer camps for individuals with various conditions.

Glossary

Table of Special Education Abbreviations

ADA	Americans with Disabilities Act
ADD	Attention Deficit Disorder
ADHD	Attention Deficit Hyperactivity Disorder
ADHD-C	Attention Deficit Hyperactivity Disorder-Combined
ADHD-HI	Attention Deficit Hyperactivity Disorder-Hyperactive/Impulsive
ADHD-I	Attention Deficit Hyperactivity Disorder-Inattentive
ADHD-NOS	Attention Deficit Hyperactivity Disorder-Not Otherwise Specified
ALDs	Assistive Listening Devices
ASD	Autistic Spectrum Disorders
ASL	American Sign Language
AT	Assistive Technology
BD	Behavior Disorders
BMR	Borderline Mentally Retarded
CAI	Computer-Assisted Instruction
CBI	Community Based Instruction
CD	Cognitive Disability—or—Conduct Disorder
CDD	Childhood Disintegrative Disorder
CIC	Clean Intermittent Catheterization
CPT	Continuos Performance Test
dB	Decibel
DI	Direct Instruction
DSM	Diagnostic and Statistical Manual
ED	Emotional Disabilities
EEG	Electroencephalograph
EHA	Education for All Handicapped Children Act
ELBW	Extremely Low Birth Weight
EMR	Educable Mentally Retarded
FAE	Fetal Alcohol Effects
FAS	Fetal Alcohol Syndrome
FC	Facilitated Communication
G-Tube	Gastrostomy Tube
IEP	Individualized Education Program
IFSP	Individualized Family Service Plan
IHCP	Individualized Health Care Plan
IPP	Individualized Program Plan
IQ	Intelligence Quotient
ITP	Individualized Transition Plan
IWRP	Individualized Written Rehabilitation Plan
LBW	Local Birth Weight

LEA	Local Education Agency
LRE	Least Restrictive Environment
MA	Mental Age
MD	Muscular Dystrophy
MMR	Mild Mental Retardation
MoMR	Moderate Mental Retardation
MR	Mental Retardation
MRI	Magnet Resonance Imaging
MS	Multiple Sclerosis
ODD	Oppositional Defiant Disorder
OHI	Other Health Impairment
OT	Occupational Therapy
PDD	Pervasive Developmental Disorder
PKU	Phenylketonuria
PLOP	Present Level of Performance
PT	Physical Therapy
SCI	Spinal Cord Injury
SD	Standard Deviation
SE	Supported Employment
SMR	Severe Mental Retardation
TA	Task Analysis
TBI	Traumatic Brain Injury
TMR	Trainable Mentally Retarded
TT	Text Telephone

ABC Model   A method of analyzing behavior involving the antecedent factors (A), behavior (B), and consequences (C) of the person's actions.

Absence Seizure   A condition characterized by a very brief loss of consciousness as if the individual is staring off into space. Also called Petit Mal Seizures.

Acceleration   Increasing the pace a student moves through a curriculum. Typically associated with students who are gifted or talented.

Acquired Hearing Loss   Hearing loss that develops after birth.

Adaptive Behavior   Skills that are important to living successful lives, such as communication, employment, self-care.

Advanced Organizers   Strategies that give students a preview of what is going to be taught.

American Sign Language (ASL)   A method of signed communication widely accepted in the United States. It is not an exact translation of spoken English.

Americans with Disability Act (ADA)   Federal legislation that prohibits the discrimination of individuals based upon their disability.

Amniocentesis   A medical procedure where amniotic fluid is examined.

Anorexia   An eating disorder characterized by an intense fear of gaining weight, distorted body image, and being significantly underweight.

Anoxia   A condition where oxygen intake is stopped and permanent damage is experienced by the brain.

Aphasia   A group of language disorders.

Applied Behavior Analysis   A systematic method of collecting and analyzing data on a student's behavior.

Asperger's Syndrome   A disorder characterized by social and behavior deficits (much like autism), but does not have the delays in language or cognitive development that autism has.

Assistive Listening Devices (ALDs)   Equipment, such as hearing aids, used to enhance the auditory abilities of people who are hard of hearing.

Assistive Technology (AT)   Services or mechanisms that assist individuals with disabilities to complete activities.

Asthma   A condition characterized by chronic difficulty in breathing.

Ataxia   A condition characterized by a lack of balance. Often associated with cerebral palsy.

Athetosis   A condition characterized by involuntary movements, such as that appear to be jerky. Often associated with cerebral palsy.

Atonic   A condition characterized by a lack of muscle tone. Often associated with cerebral palsy.

Atonic Seizures   A condition characterized by a sudden loss of muscle tone.

Attention Deficit Disorder (ADD)   An outdated term for a disorder characterized by inattentiveness (see ADHD-I).

Attention Deficit Hyperactivity Disorder (ADHD)   A group of disorders characterized by inattention, hyperactivity, or impulsivity.

Attention Deficit Hyperactivity Disorder-Combined (ADHD-C) A subtype of ADHD characterized by inattentiveness as well as hyperactivity or impulsivity.

Attention Deficit Hyperactivity Disorder-Hyperactive/Impulsive (ADHD-HI)   A subtype of ADHD characterized by hyperactivity and/or impulsivity.

Attention Deficit Hyperactivity Disorder-Inattentive (ADHD-I)   A subtype of ADHD characterized by inattentiveness.

Attention Deficit Hyperactivity Disorder-Not Otherwise Specified (ADHD-NOS)   A subtype of ADHD where individuals do not quite meet the criteria for other ADHDs, however the person's functioning is significantly impaired. Also called Pseudo-ADHD.

Audiogram   A graph used to illustrate an individual's hearing level.

Audiologist   A professional specially trained in the evaluation of hearing.

Augmentative Communication Device   Mechanisms that are used to improve an individual's ability to communicate, such as a picture board or computerized speaking device.

Aura   A sensation that people often experience just prior to having a seizure. It could involve lights getting brighter or sound getting sharper or a sudden taste in the mouth.

Authentic Assessment   Method of evaluating individuals based upon the examination of information gathered from real life activities, as opposed to information gathered via standardized tests.

Autism   A group of disorders characterized by stereotypic behavior, social aloofness, and communication deficits.

Autistic Spectrum Disorders (ASD)   A broad group of disorders characterized by autistic-like behavior in one or more areas of functioning.

Backward Chaining   A strategy for teaching where the last steps required for a task are taught first.

Basic Psychological Processes   Methods people gather information about the world around them, including auditory (hearing), kinesthetic (motor), tactile (touching), and visual (seeing).

Behavior Disorders (BD)   A broad category of disorders characterized by behavior inappropriate for the individual's age, environment, and/or situation.

Behavior Modification   A systematic approach to changing somebody's behavior, sometime by rewarding appropriate behavior and/or punishing inappropriate behavior.

Behavioral Contract   A signed agreement between a student and teacher or parent outlining the consequences (e.g., rewards and/or punishments) associated with certain behavior.

Benefit Standard   The guidelines outlined by the U.S. Supreme Court that are used to determine whether a student is receiving an "appropriate" education.

Borderline Mental Retardation (BMR)   A category of mental retardation encompassing IQs approximately between 65 and 75. Sometime used to describe individuals who have low IQs, but do not actually have mental retardation.

Braille   A system of raised dots used by individuals with vision impairments to read and write.

Bulimia   An eating disorder characterized by chronic overeating followed by purging.

Catheterization   The insertion of a tub into the urethra so that urine can be drained from the bladder of a person who cannot empty their bladder normally.

Central Nervous System   The spinal cord and brain.

Cerebral Palsy (CP)   A group of disorders characterized by poor muscle control caused by damage to the central nervous system shortly after birth or before.

Chaining   A strategy for teaching where skills required for a task are taught in order.

Childhood Disintegrative Disorder (CDD)   A group of disorders characterized by children losing previously learned skills after at least two years of normal development.

Chunking   A strategy for teaching where information is grouped together so that it is easier to remember.

Classical Conditioning   Model of teaching that focuses upon the association that a response has to a stimulus. Also called Pavlovian conditioning.

Clean Intermittent Catheterization (CIC)   A device that drains urine from the bladder.

Cleft Lip and/or Palate   A condition where the upper lip and/or roof of the mouth is deformed resulting in an opening.

Cochlear Implant   A device that surgically implanted into a person's head and enables them to hear certain sounds.

Cognition   The process of thinking.

Cognitive Disability (CD)   A disorder characterized by an impaired ability to process or interpret information. Sometimes used instead of the term "mental retardation" but could also be used to describe "learning disabilities."

Colostomy   A surgical procedure that enables a person's bowels to be emptied into an attached bag.

Community-Based Instruction (CBI)   A strategy for teaching which utilizes the community to teach skills.

Comorbidity   The occurrence of multiple disabilities that frequently go together.

Computer-Assisted Instruction (CAI)   A strategy for teaching which utilizes computer programs to teach skills.

Conduct Disorder (CD)   A disorder characterized by serious violations of society's rules.

Congenital   A condition that is present at birth.

Continuous Performance Tests (CPT)   Computer-based assessments that measure a person's attention, impulsivity, or reaction time.

Continuum of Services   The range of placement options available to students in special education.

Convulsions   Uncontrolled seizures characterized by unconsciousness and violent shaking of part or all of the body.

Criterion-Referenced Assessment   An evaluation tool that determines whether a person has mastered a particular ability or skill.

Curriculum-Based Assessment   An evaluation tool that determines whether a person has mastered the content taught.

Cystic Fibrosis   A condition characterized by the lungs becoming filled with fluid usually causing death before adulthood.

Decibel (dB)   A unit that measures the intensity of sound.

Depression   A condition characterized by a chronic state of despair not typical of the individual's usual mood.

Developmental Delay   A failure to acquire certain abilities by an age-appropriate time.

Developmental Disability   A disability that manifests itself by age 21.

Diagnostic and Statistical Manual (DSM)   A manual published by the American Psychiatric Association (APA) that is used to diagnose psychiatric conditions.

Dignity of Risk   The philosophy that individuals with disabilities should be allowed to learn from their mistakes.

Diplegia   A condition characterized by a weakness in the legs and arms, but the legs are more severely effected. Often associated with cerebral palsy.

Direct Instruction (DI)   A strategy for teaching that emphasizes drill and practice as well as immediate feedback.

Disability   A condition that impairs an individual's functioning.

Discrepancy Model   A method of identifying students with learning disabilities. Students with learning disabilities have a significant discrepancy between the students' ability and their actual performance.

Down's Syndrome   A group of disorders caused by a genetic abnormality that is characterized by poor muscle tone, flattened facial features, and sometimes mental retardation.

Dual Diagnosis   The presence of two disabilities, such as mental retardation and a behavior disorder.

Duchenne's Muscular Dystrophy   A severe form of muscular dystrophy effecting boys and characterized by a progressive weakening of the muscles. Usually results in death before adulthood.

Due Process Hearing   A formal meeting where a due process hearing officer hears all sides of a conflict typically between a school and parents.

Due Process Hearing Officer   A neutral third-party who presides over due process hearings.

Dyscalculia   A type of learning disability characterized by difficulty with math or mathematical reasoning.

Dysgraphia   A type of learning disability characterized by difficulty with hand-eye coordination, such as when writing.

Dyslexia   A type of learning disability that is characterized by difficulty in reading and writing.

Echolalia   Often a characteristic of autism where individuals repeat what they hear.

Ecological Assessment   Evaluations that examine the environments in which a person performs activities.

Educable Mentally Retarded (EMR)   An outdated term for individuals with mild mental retardation. Also called Educable Mentally Handicapped (EMH).

Education for All Handicapped Children Act (EHA)   A federal law passed in 1975. Revised and now called the Individuals with Disabilities Education Act (IDEA).

Educational Placement   The location in which a student will be taught.

Electoencephalograph (EEG)   A medical device that measures brain activity.

Emotional Disorders (ED)   Disabilities that impair the emotional functioning of individuals, such as depression and anxiety disorders.

Encoding   The ability to process language appropriately.

Epicanthic Fold   A fold of skin that covers the innermost corner of the eye. A characteristic common to individuals with Down's Syndrome.

Epidemiology The study of how frequently conditions occur within a population.

Epilepsy A broad group of disorders characterized by frequent presence of seizures.

Etiology The study of factors that cause conditions.

Evaluation Team A team of professions, family members, and other individuals who assess a child's functioning. Also called a Multi-disciplinary Team (M-Team).

Expressive Language Disorders Disorders characterized by a difficulty expressing oneself such as through speech or in writing.

Extremely Low Birth Weight (ELBW) Weight of newborns that are below 1000 grams or 2.2 pounds. Frequently associated with developmental disabilities.

Facilitated Communication (FC) A method of training individuals who are non-verbal to communicate by using a keyboard.

Febrile Seizures Seizures that are caused by high fevers.

Fetal Alcohol Effects (FAE) Disorder caused by the consumption of alcohol during pregnancy. Usually characterized by mild mental retardation.

Fetal Alcohol Syndrome (FAS) Disorder caused by the consumption of alcohol during pregnancy. Usually characterized by moderate mental retardation.

Fine Motor Skills Abilities requiring the movement of small muscle groups, such as those used when writing.

Finger Spelling A form of signed language where words are spelled out.

FM Transmission Device Technology used to help students with hearing impairments hear their teachers.

Forward Chaining A strategy for teaching where the first steps required for a task are taught first.

Fragile X Syndrome A condition caused by damage to the X-chromosome and associated with mental retardation.

Free and Appropriate Public Education (FAPE) A central component of IDEA guaranteeing students with disabilities a certain quality of education without cost to the student's family.

Full Inclusion A philosophy that all students with disabilities should be taught in the general education classroom with their non-disabled peers.

Functional Academic Skills   Skills that can be directly applied to a student's life.

Functional Analysis   A systematic study of a student's behavior in order to determine its causes and purpose.

Gastrostomy Tube (G-Tube)   A method of feeding individuals via a tube that places food directly into the intestines.

Generalization   The ability to apply knowledge learned in one setting or situation to another setting or situation.

Gifted   A term used to describe an individual with an IQ of 130 or higher.

Grief Cycle   The series of emotions that individuals and their family members often experience after learning they have a disability.

Gross Motor Skills   Abilities requiring the movement of large muscle groups, such as those used when running.

Group Homes   A residential option where small cohorts of individuals with disabilities live together in the community either in homes or apartments.

Handicap   The effects that a disability has on a person's ability to function.

Hemiplegia   A condition characterized by a weakness in the right or left side of the body. Often associated with cerebral palsy.

Hemophilia   A condition characterized by the body's inability to clot blood normally.

High IQ   A term used to describe an individual with an IQ between 119 and 129.

Home Schooling   Providing education to students at home, rather than at public or private schools.

Hoover Cane   A long white cane, usually with a red tip, that individuals with vision impairments utilize to navigate their environments.

Hypertonia   Overly tight muscles. Often a characteristic of cerebral palsy.

Hypotonia   Decreased muscle tone. Often a characteristic of cerebral palsy.

Hypoxia   A condition where oxygen in-take is slowed.

Inclusion   A term or philosophy where students with and without disabilities are educated together.

Incontinence   The inability to control the use of the bladder and/or bowel.

Individualized Education Program (IEP)   A formalized, written plan agreed to by school officials and a student's parents outlining the services that the school will provide to students in special education. Used for all students in special education between the ages of three and twenty-one.

Individualized Health Care Plan (IHCP)   A formalized plan that outlines the services that will be provided to individuals with health-care needs.

Individualized Transition Plan (ITP)   A formalized plan that outlines services and goals that will help move a student from school to adult life.

Individualized Written Rehabilitation Plan (IWRP)   A formalized plan used by vocational rehabilitation programs that outlines the services being provided to individuals with disabilities.

Individualized Family Service Plan (IFSP)   A formalized, written plan outlining the services that will be provided to children with disabilities up to three years old and their families.

Individualized Program Plan (IPP)   A formalized plan used by programs for adults with disabilities, such as sheltered workshops, that outlines the services that will be provided to individuals with disabilities.

Intelligence Quotient (IQ)   A measurement of that compares a person's mental age (MA) with their chronological age (CA) (IQ = MA/CA × 100).

Job Coach   A professional who helps train and assist workers with disabilities in supported employment programs.

Learned Helplessness   Feelings of inadequacy traditionally associated to individuals who experience frequent failures.

Learning Disabilities   A broad group of disorders characterized by difficulty in learning that of an unexplained origin.

Least Restrictive Environment (LRE)   A central component of IDEA which mandates that students with disabilities be educated with their non-disabled peers as much as possible given the student's specific needs and situation.

Legally Blind   Individuals whose best vision is 20/200 or who have a field of vision of less than 20 degrees.

Local Education Agency (LEA)   The agency that is responsible for providing special education services (e.g., the local public school system).

Low Birth Weight (LBW)   Weight of newborns that are between 3500 gram or 7.5 pounds and 1000 grams or 2.2 pounds. Frequently associated with developmental disabilities.

Low-Incidence Disability   Conditions that occur relatively infrequently, such as deaf-blind.

Macrocephaly   A condition characterized by large head sizes caused by fluid building up on the brain.

Magnet Resonance Imaging (MRI)   A medical device that produces images of a person's organs.

Magnet School   Schools for students who have are gifted and/or talented.

Mainstreaming   A philosophy or practice of placing students with disabilities in the same educational settings as their peers without disabilities for at least part of the day.

Mean   A statistical term used to describe the average score.

Mental Age (MA)   A method of expressing the intellectual development. Mental age is usually compared to chronological age.

Mental Retardation (MR)   A broad set of conditions characterized by sub-average intelligence and poor adaptive skills. Must be present by age 21.

Metacognition   The ability to think about how one learns.

Microcephaly   A condition characterized by a small head sized. Usually associated with mental retardation.

Mild Mental Retardation (MMR)   A category of mental retardation encompassing IQs approximately between 50–70 or 75.

Mnemonic   A strategy for increasing memory which traditionally uses a rhyme or acronym.

Moderate Mental Retardation (MoMR)   A category of mental retardation encompassing IQs approximately between 35 to 50.

Monoplegia   A condition characterized by a weakness in one limb. Often seen in individuals with cerebral palsy.

Multiple Intelligences   The theory that there are many different areas in which people can be skilled.

Multiple Sclerosis (MS)   A group of conditions characterized by loss of muscle control caused by scar tissue in the brain and/or spinal cord.

Muscular Dystrophy (MD)   A group of conditions characterized by a progressive weakening of the muscles. Tends to affect males more than females. Usually causes death before adulthood.

Mutism   An unwillingness or inability to speak.

Myopia   Near-sightedness. Being able to see near, but not far.

Natural Consequences   Consequences that occur as a normal result of an action.

Natural Supports   A term used to describe cues or aids for teaching skills that already exist within the environment.

Neuropsychological Assessment   A set of evaluations of a person's central nervous system.

Nondiscriminatory Evaluation   A central component of IDEA which mandates that students with disabilities be assessed in such ways that will not bias the outcome.

Normalization   A philosophy that emphasizes allowing individuals with disabilities to experience life in the same manner as individuals without disabilities.

Norm-Referenced Assessment   Evaluations where students are compared to their peers.

Occupational Therapy (OT)   A professional trained to assess and improve an individual's fine motor functioning.

Ophthalmologist   A medical professional specializing in the assessment and treatment of eye disorders.

Oppositional Defiant Disorder (ODD)   A type of behavior disorder that is characterized by hostile or disobedient actions towards authority figures.

Optometrist   A professional specializing in the measurement of vision and the prescription of corrective lenses.

Other Health Impairment (OHI)   A broad category of disorders that are not included within other disability categories, such as asthma.

Otitis Media   An infection of the middle ear that can cause hearing loss.

Palsy   Muscular weakness or paralysis

Paraplegia   A condition characterized by limited use of the arms.

Paraprofessional   A teacher's aide.

Peer Tutoring   A teaching strategy where students help teach other students.

Perinatal   Occurring at birth

Peripheral Vision   The outermost area of an individual's visual field.

Personal Futures Planning   A technique of planning for somebody's future by discussing their long- and short-range goals and dreams.

Pervasive Developmental Disorder (PDD)   A broad category of disorders that are characterized by impairments in communication, social skills, and stereotypic behavior. Autism is an example of a pervasive developmental disorder.

Phenylketonuria (PKU)   A condition characterized by inability for a person's body to metabolize various proteins causing mental retardation and damage to the central nervous system.

Phonological Awareness   The ability to recognize the sounds associated with letters and combinations of letters

Physical Therapy (PT)   A professional trained to assess and improve an individual's gross motor functioning.

Pica   An eating disorder characterized by the consumption of nonfood material such as dirt.

Portfolio Assessment   A method of evaluation students by collecting samples of their work.

Postnatal   Occurring after birth

Prader-Willi Syndrome   A condition characterized by compulsive eating, obesity, mental retardation, and poor social development.

Prenatal   Occurring before birth.

Prereferral   Point during which teachers attempt to address a student's difficulties prior to referring the student for a formal evaluation for special education.

Present Level of Performance (PLOP)   The section of the Individualized Education Program that discusses the student's current strengths and areas of concern.

Profound Mental Retardation (PMR)   A category of mental retardation encompassing IQs approximately 20 and below.

Prostheses   Artificial replacements body parts, such as false legs.

Psychologist   A professional specializing in the assessment of individuals.

Pull-Out Program   A model of special education that emphasizes placing a student with disabilities primarily in the general education classroom but bringing them to a resource room when they need help.

Quadriplegia A condition characterized by a limited use of both arms and legs.

Receptive Language Disorders A condition characterized by difficulties processing incoming information.

Referral Point during which teachers officially refer a student for a nondiscriminatory evaluation in order to determine eligibility for special education.

Related Services Services not automatically part of special educational programs that students with disabilities require in order to benefit from special education. Transportation and counseling are examples of related services.

Reliability The consistency that results are obtained over time and across evaluators.

Resource Room A school environment where students with disabilities can get extra help when they need it.

Rett's Syndrome A condition prevalent only in females characterized by autistic-like tendencies and progressive neurological deterioration.

Savant A condition in which an individual with mental retardation displays dramatic strengths or abilities.

Schizophrenia A group of disorders characterized by psychotic hallucinations and delusions.

Scoliosis A condition where there is a lateral curve to the spine.

Section 504 The portion of the Rehabilitation Act of 1974 that prohibits programs receiving federal funding from discriminating against people with disabilities.

Self-Advocacy The ability to promote your own rights and interests.

Self-Contained Classroom An environment where students with disabilities are educated with other students who have disabilities. Students without disabilities are not included within these environments.

Self-Determination The ability to make decisions regarding your own life.

Self-Injurious Behavior (SIB) Actions which cause injury to oneself, such as head banging.

Self-Stimulation Inappropriate behavior which occupies the person's senses, such as hand flapping. Often seen in individuals with autism.

Severe Mental Retardation (SMR)   A category of mental retardation encompassing IQs approximately between 35 and 20.

Shaken Baby Syndrome   A condition characterized by brain damage caused by the violent shaking of small children.

Sheltered Workshops   Vocational programs for individuals with severe disabilities that involves working within non-inclusive, non-community-based settings. Also called Segregated Workshops.

Shunt   A surgically inserted tube that drains fluid from a persons head usually to the abdomen. Often used for individuals with hydrocephaly.

Signed English   A form of sign language through which English is translated manually exactly as it spoken.

Spasticity   A condition characterized by hyper-rigid muscle tone. Often seen in individuals with cerebral palsy.

Special Education   A federally mandated program to meet the individual needs students with qualifying disabilities

Speech Pathologist   A professional trained to treat language and speech disorders.

Spina Bifida   A group of conditions characterized by malformed spinal column.

Spinal Cord Injury (SCI)   A condition characterized by damage to the spinal cord.

Standard Deviation (SD)   A statistical term used to describe the variation of scores from the average score.

Stereotypical Behavior   Repetitive acts that are inappropriate for the person's age and situation. Examples of stereotypical behaviors include rocking back and forth, hand flapping, and twirling objects.

Strabismus   A condition characterized by an improper alignment of the eyes.

Supported Employment (SE)   A vocational program for individuals with severe disabilities that involves working competitively within the community.

Talented   A term used to describe an individual with unusual strengths in certain areas, such as sports or art.

Task Analysis (TA)   A systematic break down of the steps required to complete a task.

Tay-Sachs Disease   A condition characterized by physical and mental deterioration. Usually leading to death by age 6.

Text Telephone (TT)   Telephones that produce conversations in writing.

Time Out   A method of correcting inappropriate behavior by temporarily removing the offending student from the immediate environment.

Token Economy   A system of providing immediate feedback regarding behavior. For example, students who are behaving appropriately might be given play money that could later be used to purchase items or privileges. The money could also be taken away for inappropriate behavior.

Tonic-Clonic Seizures   A condition where individuals experience sudden loss of consciousness and body control. Also called grand mal seizures.

Tourette's Disorder   A condition characterized by uncontrollable vocal and motor tics.

Tracheostomy   A surgical opening in an individual's throat through which the person can breathe through a tube.

Trainable Mentally Retarded (TMR)   An outdated term for individuals with moderate to severe mental retardation. Also called Trainable Mentally Handicapped (TMH).

Transition-Related Services   Activities mandated by IDEA that prepare students for their adult life, such as their employment.

Traumatic Brain Injury (TBI)   Damage to the brain resulting from an external force.

Triplegia   A condition characterized by a weakness in three limbs. Often seen in individuals with cerebral palsy.

Tunnel Vision   A condition where an individual's field of vision is reduced significantly.

Turner's Syndrome   A condition characterized by physical abnormalities, such as a lack of secondary sexual characteristics, webbed neck, learning and behavior difficulties. Prevalent only in females.

Ultrasonography   A medical procedure used to examine a fetus.

Validity   The accuracy to which assessment devices measure what they are suppose to measure.

Virtual Schools   Providing education to students via the internet or computer-based applications. Usually used as part of a home schooling program.

Whole Language   Strategies using naturally occurring opportunities to learn reading and writing.

Zero Reject   The philosophy presented in IDEA which states that no student who qualifies for special education can be excluded from special education services.

Bibliography

American Psychiatric Association (2000). *Diagnostic and statistical manual of mental disorders* (4th ed.). Washington, DC: American Psychiatric Association.

Barkley, R.A. (2000). *Taking charge of ADHD: The complete, authoritative guide for parents.* New York: Guilford.

Bennis, W.G., & Shepard, H.A. (1956). A theory of group development. *Human Relations, 9,* 415–437.

Cimera, R.E. (2002). *Making ADHD a gift: Teaching Superman how to fly.* Lanham, MD: Scarecrow Education Press.

Fombonne, E. (1999). The epidemiology of autism: A review. *Psychological Medicine, 29,* 769–786.

Forness, S.R., & Knitzer, J. (1992). A new proposed definition and terminology to replace "serious emotional disturbance" in IDEA. *School Psychology Review, 21,* 12–20.

Friend, M., & Cook, L. (2000). *Interactions: Collaboration skills for school professionals.* New York: Longman.

Hallahan, D.P. & Kauffman, J.M. (2000). *Exceptional learners: Introduction to special education* (8th ed.). Boston: Allyn and Bacon.

Hunt, N., & Marshall, K. (1999). *Exceptional children and youth* (2nd ed.). Boston: Houghton Mifflin.

Johnson, D.W., & Johnson, F.P. (1997). *Joining together: Group theory and group skills* (6th ed.). Boston: Allyn and Bacon.

Kubler-Ross, E. (1969). *Death and dying.* New York: Macmillan.

McIntyre, T. & Forness, S.R. (1996). Is there a new definition yet or are our kids still seriously emotionally disturbed? *Beyond Behavior, 7*(3), 4–9.

National Center for Health Statistics (2002). *Fast stats: A to Z* [online]. www.cdc.gov/nchs.

Piirto, J. (1999). *Talented children and adults: Their development and education* (2nd ed.). Upper Saddle River, NJ: Merrill.

Scholtes, P.R., Joiner, B.L., & Streibel, B.J. (1996). *The team handbook* (2nd ed.). Madison, WI: Joiner Associates Inc.

Tuckman, B. & Jensen, M. (1977). Stages of small group development revisited. *Group and Organizational Studies, 2,* 419–427.

Tuckman, B. (1965). Developmental sequence in small groups. *Psychological Bulletin, 63,* 384–399.

Turnbull, A.P., & Turnbull, H.R. (2001). *Families, professionals, and exceptionality: Collaborating for empowerment* (4th ed.). Upper Saddle River, NJ: Merrill.

Turnbull, R., Turnbull, A., Shank, M., Smith, S., & Leal, D. (2002). *Exceptional lives: Special education in today's schools* (3rd ed.). Upper Saddle River, NJ: Merrill.

U.S. Census Bureau (2000). *Population report.* Washington, DC: U.S. Government Printing Office.

U.S. Department of Education (1999). *To Assure the Free Appropriate Public Education of All Children with Disabilities: Twenty-First Annual Report to Congress.* Washington, DC: U.S. Government Printing Office.

Wehman, P., Sherron, P.D., & West, M.D. (1997). Education of Individuals with Disabilities. In P. Wehman (Ed.). *Exceptional Individuals in School, Community, and Work* (pp. 3–57). Austin, TX: Pro-Ed.

Index

About the Author

Robert Evert Cimera taught individuals with severe and multiple disabilities for several years prior to completing his Ph.D. in Special Education from the University of Illinois at Champaign-Urbana. He currently is an assistant professor at the University of Wisconsin at Oshkosh where he studies Attention Deficit Hyperactivity Disorders (ADHD), teaches pre-service teachers, and presents around the nation on how to make ADHD a gift. He can be reached at robertcimera@yahoo.com.